BLOGG___

PROFIT IN

2020:

10,000/month ultimate guide – Make a Passive Income Fortune using Effective SEO Techniques & Affiliate Marketing Secrets leveraging your contents on YouTube & Social Media

By

Ronald Roberts

Table of Content

Introduction: Why Blogging? 7

Chapter 1: Blogging for Profit 10

Sam's Story 10

Why Start in 2019? 11

How to Turn a Blog into Profit? 13
Choosing the Right Niche 13

Creating Content for your Blog 15

Chapter 2: Setting up a Blog-The Basics 17

WordPress-why it is the best? 17
WordPress is Easy to Use 17
Ready to Use Themes and Plugins 18
Excellent for a Static Site............................18
Easy to Use with Your Mobile Phone 18
Compatibility with All Popular Web Browsers 19
Unique, But Intuitive Look............................19
Buying the Domain 20
HostGator 20
NameCheap..20
Hover 21
GoDaddy 21
Gandi...21
Dreamhost 21
Name.com 22
1and1 22
Network Solutions 22
Hostinger 22
Flippa 23
Domain.com..23

Bluehost 23

Wix.com 23

Web.com 24

Installing WordPress 24

Getting Web Server Access 24

Get a Reliable Text Editor 24

Get an FTP Client...25

Select the Web Browser to Use 25

Options to Use for WordPress Installation 26

Installing Manually with FTP.................................27

How to Link your Domain with WordPress...............29

Installing the Right Theme.....................................31

Page VS Post 33

Tags, Ranking, and SEO 34

What are Tags and How to use Them in the Correct
Way?..34

The Importance of Search Engine Optimization on
Page (SEO on Page) 34

How Google Ranks Sites in 2019: Top Ranking Factors
....35

Content Quality...36

Quality Backlinks..36

Secured Sites (A shift from HTTP to HTTPS)............37

Page speed...37

Webpage Content Length 38

Mobile friendly Websites..38

Domain age 39

Google Updates and How to survive them................39

Authority...40

Trust..40

Relevance 41

How to Structure your Blog for Easy and Automatic SEO 41

Avoid Duplicating Content and Giving Searchers What They Want.. 42

The Importance of the Sitemap 43

Usability 43

Responsive 44

The Importance of Link Building: Why is linking building so important? 44

Paying to get Link on Website with Authority 44

How to Acquire Links and What to Avoid in Link Building.. 45

Chapter 3: Other Monetization Methods Part 1 .46

Affiliate Marketing..46

Most Popular Affiliate Programs................................. 50

Choosing products or a price range for affiliate products 54

How to pick up the products-services that sell the most 59

Chapter 4: Other Monetization Methods 2........64

Direct Email Marketing.....................................64

The Importance of Email Marketing: create lists and advertise related products 65

Creating an email list outside your blog.................... 66

What should your email send include? 69

Keeping Subscribers engaged 69

Chapter 5: Other Monetization Methods 3.........72

Advertising on your Blogs 72

Types of Ads and Methods of Using Them 74

Publishing Contextual Ads 74

Using text link ads 75

Placing Impression Ads 75

Publishing Sponsored Reviews and Paid Posts.......... 77

Guest Posts... 77

Placing your own Ads selling your Products-services 78

Displaying Ads in your Blog's Feed 80

Selling Ad Space Directly.. 81

Chapter 6: Using Google and Social Media for Profit **83**

Google AdSense **83**

Google AdWords **84**

Using Social Media **85**

Create a profile on the main social Networks ..88

Facebook 88

How it works 88

Marketing and Advertising on Facebook 91

Instagram... 92

Twitter... 94

YouTube 95

Patreon.. 113

Reddit & Quora 114

Social Media Strategy **114**

Chapter 7: In Conclusion **118**

Staying on top of your niche and popular with advertisers **118**

Resources for Bloggers-as suggested by award-winning Blogger Raelyn Tan. You can find her at her blog **123**

Introduction: Why Blogging?

Blogging has gained traction for people seeking passive income in the past decade. This is because the internet is readily available in almost all parts of the world. The speeds are also very good to sustain heavy usage by many customers. Many internet providers are doing a good job in innovating which encourages a lot of users. A blog is a website in which the author passes information in written form. The messages are passed using blog posts where the author can pick almost anything to talk about. With more and more people getting most of their information from the internet, there is someone looking for whatever you want to talk about.

With so much information online, your content is bound to get buried in the noise. The only thing that will separate you from the rest is if you infuse some of your personality and opinions. Everything that we shall discuss in this book has been done and will continue being done, therefore, you have to make sure your personal perspective comes out in the way you write or conduct this business called blogging.

The main aim of blogging is to create an intimate communication between yourself and your reader. There is a comment section in every blog where the reader can leave their questions, thoughts, and feedback on the topic in the blog post. The readers that will follow your blog are people interested in what you have to say, and you must do your best to be authentic and trustworthy so that they can support your business. You have to ensure that you create a loyal fanbase who will support any business venture you may want to start.

Many people have argued that it may be too late to start blogging in 2019 because there are way too many people blogging nowadays, but I beg to differ. There will always be a gap in what you can offer in any field even if it is saturated. There is always something you can contribute, either new or additional. Another myth is that you need to be a master or expert in the topic you want to write about. You don't need any prior knowledge or to be a master of writing at all. You just need to be able to conduct research on your niche or topic and be able to give true, accurate, and useful information. Once you do that, boom you are an expert in the area that people will respect and seek out.

All the tools you need are available online and there are many courses, books, video, and many other resources that are out there for beginners. They explain step-by-step ways on how you can move from amateur to expert in almost any field or niche. Does it sound too easy? Don't be skeptical, just realistic. Blogging requires patience and dedication. There is no overnight success in making money blogging, especially if you don't do it consistently.

The main thing you will need to have in this business is a passion for both learning and the topic you choose to focus on. These two things will keep you motivated even if you don't make money the first couple of months or more. The reason passion is very important is because readers will see through your act very fast and you shall miss out on some loyal readers. Basically, as a PASSIONATE blogger, you are set to reach out to other passionate fans or curious novices of your niche. Strive to hit the loyal fan ratio of 500 hundred people that will give you just 20 dollars per month, and trust me, there are many ways of doing that!

Read on to discover them.

Chapter 1: Blogging for Profit

Sam's Story

Sam loved food, in fact so much so, that she was over 300lbs by the time she was 35. She knew something had to change, so she started on the Keto Diet. She was hooked as the weight melted off her and all her blood and medical tests came back normal (unlike the prediabetic state prior to her weight loss). She had to tell people, so she started a blog. It started as a daily record of her weight loss journey, noting what she ate and how she felt. Within 3 months, she had 2k followers that were logging in several times a week. Some wanted to do more, so she partnered with AdSense to monetize her site in hopes she could work out of her day job and help people full time.

It went fairly well, but she was only generating about 300 dollars per month with her 2k followers. So, she started adding special posts for those that wished to support her on the social media site Patreon. The posts were emailed to them for as little as 1 dollar per month. She also started a Facebook group for her followers to meet and talk about their own struggles and a YouTube Channel to turn her Blogs into VLOGS. Within 3 months, she had an additional 3k followers between all the sites. She finally wrote a Keto Cookbook (using the recipes she posted on her blog and others she created), as well as a Keto 101 e-book. She offered them for paid download on all her sites and on Kindle. Within 6 months her income had jumped to 10k a month and she was able to devote full-time efforts to her following. Soon she will hire a freelancer to help her manage her sites and will start appearing at Keto and

Weight Loss conferences/organizations for paid speaking gigs and sales of the hard copy versions of her books and t-shirts she created.

Want to be like Sam, read on.

Why Start in 2019?

Don't listen to the naysayers that whine about if you are not already established as a niche expert, then don't even bother, because your field is all saturated. Shake that off and remember that trends change and evolve and so do the needs of the knowledge seeking public. Therefore, I guarantee that you can bring a fresh perspective to any niche and package it in a way that is more appealing than what is already out there. So, keeping that in mind lets go over why blogging is a worthwhile pursuit in 2019.

1. **You get to make money from any part of the world.**

There are literally no limitations as to where or when you can blog. As long as you have internet and a portable computer, or even a smartphone or tablet, you are set to start. As long as you have created a great blog that has a loyal following, you can even make money as you sleep. Some bloggers become digital nomads because they have understood that blogging gives them the freedom to travel and still make money. Some of them even live on full time blogging because they earn enough money to sustain their lifestyles. There are literally no limits to the money you can earn, if you act smartly.

2. Tell your story online

Blogging isn't just about making money for everyone. Some people find it therapeutic to put their life experiences, real or fictional stories, and other personal information on the internet. Some stories are meant to inspire, educate, and stimulate the mind and need to be shared where everyone can see. There is also a need for escapism for many people, so they turn to the blogs and vlogs (which we will talk about later) of people living different types of lives to experience the adventure they don't see in their own lives. There is a wide audience that is meant to enjoy these stories and appreciate the candor.

3. Put yourself, your brand or business out there

The importance of setting up a website and social media in today's business world cannot be understated. This is because people want to see what you are all about before they commit to buying from you. Google, Bing, and Yahoo searches are some of the ways in which people discover new people, products, and the services that they may have been searching for. In addition, searches on Facebook (with 1.8 billion users), Instagram/Twitter (with millions of trending hashtags), and YouTube (the 2nd largest search engine in the world) are another necessity for modern branding. All of these methods can be used to sell your main product and blog. A blog just makes it easier to sell yourself to potential readers and clients, because it allows your followers to get to know you more than just having a website. They see you as a real person, not just a business owner.

4. Build an online community

You may never meet some of the people who share the same interests as you from other parts of the world, but this is easy with blogs. People are able to share and discuss on the topics they are interested in and support each other thanks to a community created by a certain blog. Blogging allows you to learn from other people as well as share the knowledge you already have. If you share your contact information, you may make some lifelong friends thanks to blogging.

How to Turn a Blog into Profit?

Choosing the Right Niche

It is important to remember that even if you are passionate about a certain topic, it may not be as profitable as other topics. This is unfortunate but true. You can blog about anything you want as long as you are just doing it for fun. However, if you want to make money, you have to choose the right niche that people are interested in. The same applies for what you are an expert in. Blogging for profit is dependent on the audience rather than what you are good at. You will be very fortunate if the area you are an expert in and are passionate about is what people are looking for online. Working hard at a niche that isn't profitable won't make any difference at all.

Some of the most profitable niches include:

1. **Health and fitness** – People have recently joined the health and fitness bandwagon and are looking for natural ways to stay healthy and fit. You can choose topics like healthy meals with basic foods or

something more extreme like Keto/Carnivore/Low Carb Lifestyle, Intermittent Fasting, or Plant Based. Also, some other topics might be simple exercises one can do at home to complicated gym routines, and natural supplements or vitamins for better health etc.

2. **Personal finance** – topics like how to make passive income, side hustles that make you money, how to budget your income, how to make money from home or paying off debt.

3. **Parenting** -young parents are clamoring for help in raising children, so any experienced parent or caretaker has a wealth of information to offer.

4. **Holistic or Natural Medicine**-there is a market for those who wish to take a more natural approach to healing. Topics like reflexology, Chiropractic, Eastern Healing for the physical body or spiritual concepts like the Law of Attraction offer a wealth of possible readers.

5. **Home Schooling**-the home-schooling trend is fast accelerating and advice or curriculums for better methods are always a hot commodity.

To pick the right niche which you can focus all your efforts in, you have to consider several factors:

o People have to show an interest in the niche, whether rational or irrational e.g. Bullet journaling.

o You have a solution to people's problem.

o People should be willing to spend their money on

products or services related to the niche.

Creating Content for your Blog

If you are interested in blogging for profit, I am sure you have already come across the phrase, "Content is King". The reason why this statement is quoted in every blogging for profit book, blog, or course is because, content is the only thing that will separate you from your competition. Whatever niche you pick, there is probably someone who already beat you to it. That's not to discourage you because readers are always looking for engaging, mind stimulating, and useful information out there. The only tool you have to do this is the content on your blog. There are three things that you might want to keep in mind before creating any content for your blog:

o What you are brainstorming and thinking about may not necessarily be what people are looking for.

o Use frameworks that are already working when creating content.

o There is nothing new that your post has to offer the reader, instead you have to put a new and interesting slant on it.

I don't mean to discourage you but to help you get rid of the "know-it-all" mentality so that you can succeed. You are starting from scratch when you choose to start blogging and it should reflect as such in the way you come up with content for your blog. You have to give more importance to the needs of readers rather than your own. I repeat, this doesn't apply if you are blogging for fun or personal use, but to for profit blogging only. Write down your personal thoughts and ideas and after you have researched, you can find areas that need those ideas.

Remember these three important levels when you are trying to create content for your blog:

- o Find the most popular topics in your chosen niche and stick to them.

· Research and learn the frameworks that other successful bloggers have already established and use them when creating content. This saves you from making silly mistakes that could lead to the slow growth of your blog.

- o The content you deliver should provide useful information that readers are interested in. It doesn't have to be unique (but that helps), just valuable.

Now how do you go about the technical or physical production of your blog, there are several options online for blogging sites or extensions for already established websites. In chapter two I will suggest the easiest and most straightforward site for producing blogs.

Chapter 2: Setting up a Blog-The Basics

WordPress-why it is the best?

WordPress is the best option for any blogger when they want their presence felt online, as it is the most used and has the widest reach via search engines and word of mouth. This is a CMS or Content Management System that will run your website smoothly and efficiently. It comes with different features, templates, and tools that ease the process of customization. With so many potential choices in WordPress, you will thrive online and be able to adjust to new trends very easily. The CMS is free (if you do a direct download of the software and use it to set up your own site or integrate it into an existing site, the online version and use of the WordPress site to host your blog is $2.75 a month), yet strong and flexible to accommodate your eCommerce needs. Read on to see why WordPress is your number one option as a blogger:

WordPress is Easy to Use

WordPress is easy to use, even for beginners. The first time you have to use any software, you might feel intimidated. But this CMS makes creating your first website easy despite not having any experience with such platforms, as it is a click and do type of set up.

There is no coding involved, and even the admin dashboard comes in straightforward language. Navigation is smooth whether you are looking for the best themes, installing plugins, customizing settings, or writing content.

For the seasoned internet gurus, the simplicity of WordPress should not turn you off, as it will enable you to do more, quicker than doing your own coding. This is a powerful CMS that will enable you to customize your website the way you want.

Ready to Use Themes and Plugins

The outlook of a blog is determined by the theme you choose to use. The theme is not customizable in every aspect, but it does help you get a unique look. The elements you add help your blog stand out among others with the same theme. However, it shouldn't be overdone because excessive customization can affect how the theme is presented by different web browsers and screen resolutions.

Excellent for a Static Site

WordPress is updated periodically and therefore makes the best platform for a static website. This CMS will help your blog rank high with the search engines. If you have been marketing your blog using a static HTML website, moving to WordPress will bring many changes.

This is due to the platform's plugins that make your website easy to rank high. Besides, this CMS' dashboard does not require a tech guru to make any necessary changes. Furthermore, it allows easy integration of your site with different social media platforms. Nothing increases your chances of appearing on the first page of a search page more than a social media connection.

Easy to Use with Your Mobile Phone

Mobile users outnumber other types of devices by a huge

margin. Those who go online via a smartphone every day are more than those who use desktops, tablets, or laptops. So, if your website is not mobile friendly, you will be losing big business opportunities. WordPress takes the guesswork out of this process by offering a wide array of themes and templates that are mobile compatible. It makes adopting a blog that offers a mobile friendly web design very easy and a built-in function of the software. This simply means your design will adjust automatically to display content clearly regardless of the mobile device's size, via WordPress.

Compatibility with All Popular Web Browsers

WordPress is compatible with all the major web browsers, with no known issues or errors. People use different web browsers, depending on their devices and location, so your blog should be strategically placed where everyone can access it. Choose a theme that will appear as intended and avoid any that might look too small, too big, or will rearrange all of the elements when viewed with some browsers.

WordPress has a compatibility that you can use to see how your blog looks in its mobile and web version when viewed using various web browsers. The top web browsers include Mozilla Firefox, Internet Explorer, Opera, Safari and Chrome.

Unique, But Intuitive Look

The intuitiveness of WordPress is related to its customizability. It allows you to choose to customize themes to get a unique look by using a plethora of colors, design, and layout. As a blogger, you know the brand you want and communicate it to your readers via the look of your site.

The easy to navigate WordPress site will ensure your visitors will not struggle to find the icons to click. The links and all navigation buttons are laid out clearly without any distracting ads. Just because WordPress allows you to create something distinctive, your site does not become complicated or complex for users, as the built-in functions keep the site smooth and fully visible.

Buying the Domain

Finding a domain name is a primary step when creating a website. Where you buy and register the domain name will not affect your WordPress in any way. You just choose the site with which you would like to register your site (a list is below), based on the important things like if their price is within your budget, if you like their interface or if they have extra services that want to access quickly. You can buy your domain from any of the following companies, without worrying about the compatibility of your blog.

HostGator

HostGator is one of the popular domain registrars. They also offer hosting after you have purchased your area. The hosting packages vary from as low as $3 per month. They have high-quality services, which include 99.99% uptime. By buying your domain from them and seeking their hosting services, your blog will start its journey online on a good note.

NameCheap

Namecheap is easy to use and incredibly intuitive. They

are excellent in domain management services, which is usually very helpful. The domains are reasonably priced, plus you get a free DNS service combine with WHOIS protection. If you want tight security, this domain registrar offers SSL encryption.

Hover

Hover is an accredited online registrar, launched in 2009. It is an offshoot one of the biggest ICANN accredited registrars online known as Tucows Inc. Hover is straightforward making domain registration easy via a seamless process. They also have superb support, and their pricing depends on the top level of the domain you choose to use.

GoDaddy

GoDaddy is a famous domain registrar that also offers web hosting services. They are a big company and the largest name registrar worldwide. Apart from selling domains, they also have other services to support websites online depending on what you need. Their annual cost for a domain is $14.99, but sometimes they have incredible offers where you can buy a domain for as low as $0.90

Gandi

Gandi is a great place to buy your domain. It has been in the business for two decades and they have no hidden fees. Their packages are straightforward, and you will not be asked to make extra payments. To register a domain with them will cost you $15.50 and transfer charges are $8.00.

Dreamhost

Dreamhost was established in 1997 and today, it offers

both domain registration and web hosting services. They have features such as free privacy services for your domain and ability to control the settings of your domain.

Name.com

Name.com has been in domain registration business for years. Besides selling domains, they also offer web hosting, email services, and a website builder. Using their unique feature to search domains, you can see all the domain extensions available for your domain. They have different services on a single platform, and their prices are reasonable. Both .net and .com extensions will cost you $12.99 and a .org is $10.99

1and1

1and1 manages millions of domains. It has been in the field for a long time and works perfectly for online users looking for pocket-friendly services. For all first-time users looking for domains to buy, 1and1 offers each at $0.9. However, renewal goes to $14.99. They do not have additional registration and ICANN fees, and so the price is constant.

Network Solutions

Network Solutions offers domains and web hosting services according to your needs. A domain name will not cost you more than $9.99. They have customer support, which is available any time of the day and will help you navigate their platform if you need some assistance.

Hostinger

Hostinger is a well-established domain registrar and web hosting company. Their pricing attracts many online users with .coms available at $11 annually. The less known domain extension cost $0.99. Anyone looking for affordable domain registration, Hostinger has a solution.

Flippa

Flippa is a marketplace dealing with websites and domains. They usually have many domains on sale and great discounts where you can buy a domain name for less than a dollar. If you are getting started online as a blogger, Flippa is excellent. It has a solid backlink profile that will increase your ability to rank high with search engines.

Domain.com

Domain.com targets small businesses with various affordable web hosting options. They also have useful tools for blogs and small businesses. Their loyal customers get huge discounts. There are coupons to allow other users to enjoy discounts when buying domains from Domain.com.

Bluehost

Bluehost is a big name in the web hosting industry. You can register your domain name with them and also use the hosting services. With all services on a single platform, Bluehost helps you get started with your blog immediately. Their stellar support service ensures your questions and requests are attended to immediately regardless of the time.

Wix.com

Wix is a simple straightforward site, where you can buy your domain and host it there if you choose. The rates are very reasonable, and they have a plethora of options like click and build sites or full integration with a prebuilt site using WordPress.

Web.com

Web.com is very similar to Wix and offers domains a low prices and full web hosting and integration if needed.

Installing WordPress

WordPress is easy to install, and the whole process does not take more than five minutes to accomplish. There are some web hosts with tools that enable automatic installation of WordPress so the process there would be a bit different, but the five basic things that you must do regardless of the methods you will use to install your WordPress are:

Getting Web Server Access

Before installing WordPress, get web hosting services from a reliable company. This is what enables your blog to go online and reach your readers. So, select any company from the list above that sell domains and also offer web hosting services.

Get a Reliable Text Editor

Text editors are many, and a good example is the Notepad (which is free and preinstalled on most PCs). They allow you to access and edit text files without the need to format. It will ease the procedure of editing once you're in the WordPress files. Using word processors with their formatting such as Microsoft Word will cause damage to the codes and files. But in case you wish to use something other than Notepad, here is a list of both free and purchased text editors, just Google them for information:

1. Notepad++

2. Coda

3. TextWrangler

4. Sublime Text

5. Textmate

6. Atom

7. BBEdit

8. UltraEdit

9. Vim

10. Brackets

11. Coffee Cup HTML Editor

12. Espresso

Get an FTP Client

This is the method to use when downloading, uploading and managing WordPress files on the server. Basically, it is a method to upload, download, and manage files on a (usually private) server, but it is not needed if you choose to use a hosting provider since they will take of it.

Select the Web Browser to Use

This is simple and any web browser is good enough to download and install your WordPress.

Download WordPress-The Latest Version. Visit the

WordPress site to make sure you only download their latest version.

Options to Use for WordPress Installation

1. Automatic Installation

Bloggers are lucky because some web hosting providers provide automatic installation of WordPress. Bluehost and Dreamhost are some of these hosts and are the best options if you are just starting out. You do not need to be an experienced web developer; if you get stuck, you can contact their support service.

2. Installing WordPress on a Computer

Installing WordPress on your computer is possible. It is not common with bloggers because most of them want to reach many people. Installing WordPress in your computer means that it will be available to you and other people cannot access it.

3. cPanel Installation

The cPanel installation is one of the best options for bloggers. You must have some basic web technical skills to install a tailor-made WordPress site. The hosting company gives access to cPanel. After signing up, you can use the credentials to access the cPanel dashboard and locate the section called "auto-installers."

Once you click on the auto-install button, go to the WordPress icon and click. You are redirected to another page where you will see "Install Now," click on it. Follow instructions; the first one is to enter your domain name. This page looks similar regardless of the auto-installer or cPanel you choose to use.

"http" is the default under "Protocol" and the best to stick with. However, if you have SS certificate installed, you should use "https." Besides, you will be given an option to enter "directory." Most people opt to leave it blank so that WordPress installs in their primary domain. When left blank, the URL appears like this: www.mysite.com. If you choose to enter, it will read this: www.mysite.cm/blog. It means WordPress will be installed in a small part of your website.

You also have the option to include your business name where it reads the business name and give a small description of what you do under where it reads the purpose of your website. You will find these options under the icon labeled "Site Settings". However, you can always change these details later if you want to.

Finally, go to the admin page and fill the necessary information. You need an email, admin username, and a password. Provide answers for all questions asked and click install.

To reach the backend of your site, you use www.mysite.com/wp-admin. This is the point where you edit admin details when needed.

Installing Manually with FTP

With so many web hosting companies offering WordPress Automatic installation and the auto-installers available in the cPanel, there is no need to install this software manually with FTP. However, it is possible to install your WordPress if that is what you want.

Step 1

Before you get started, you must have an FTP program like the FileZilla or SmartFTP. Start by completing the first five tasks before installation begins.

Step 2

Unzip the file from WordPress and upload to the public directory. It will appear like this: public_html.

Step 3

Move t to CPanel to the "MySQL Databases. It is easy to spot it; all cPanels have the same look. Create a database and next is the "user" creation for the MYSQL account. Enter the username and a password and click on "Create User."

Step 4

After creating the user, include their details and indicate the database where you want to add them. Move on to the next page and check the privileges you want to give them.

Step 5

At this point, the FTP transfer is complete. Go to your domain and complete the installation process. If you're prompted to select the language to use when you check your domain, installation is successful.

Step 6

You are almost done; this step requires to enter your Database Name, Your Username, Password, Database Host, and the Table Prefix. Click on "Run the Install. Then you have to provide your WordPress admin with information such as the username, site title, email, and password. All these are the ones that you created when installing your WordPress.

Finally, you are done, so simply click "Install WordPress." At this point, you can log in into your site using your username and password, and your site is ready for use

How to Link your Domain with WordPress

Once your blog is on WordPress.com, you can get your domain to help you brand the site. The free website's address is the blog's name.WordPress.com, which will not have a significant impact on your brand exposure.

However, to add your domain in WordPress is not free; you have to pay $14.97 yearly for a new domain and $9.97 annually to map a domain that you already own.

Here is How to Link the Domain

Login in your site and on the dashboard, click Upgrades and choose Domains.

Enter the subdomain or domain in the text box and click on the button labeled add domain to blog.

WordPress has to confirm the availability of the domain before registration. If it is, you get a registration form to fill after that hit the Register Domain button.

For a domain that is already in use, you get the following results:

If the domain is yours, you have the option to map it. So, go to the domain registrar account where you can change your server name like this:

NS1.WordPress.COM

NS2WordPress.COM

The DNS settings of the domain may look different. This is determined by the registrar you chose to use. But, you get something like this:

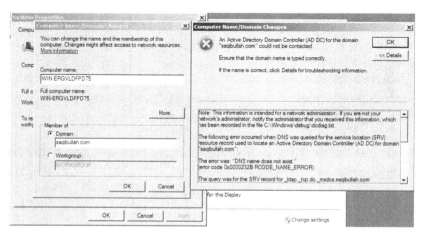

For a subdomain like blog.mysite.com, you need CNAME record. But, for this domain linking, you have to contact your registrar's customer support. Make sure you replace the subdomain, blog name and domain in the CNAME record.

Click *Try Again*, once you have the correct settings. However, you have to wait for some time for the DNS settings to update. When it's done, your screen should show you this:

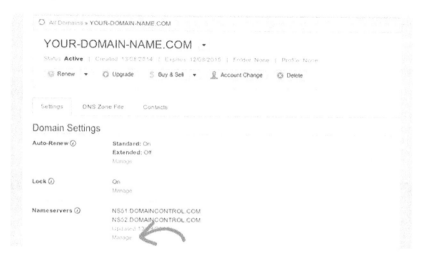

Hit the *Map Domain* button and the domain will be added to your WordPress blog.

At this point, you should pay for registration or mapping. Choose method of payment and follow the steps.

After payment, try your new domain and it will definitely open your blog.

Installing the Right Theme

Installing the right theme should be a hard task. You may

want to check out a few before you settle for the best. Every time you activate a new theme, it changes the outlook of your site immediately.

There are four ways to install a theme in your WordPress site:

- o Using access via admin area of WordPress

- o Download the theme to your computer

- o Accessing FTP

- o Use of phpMyadmin

The easiest way of installing a free WordPress theme is through the dashboard. They have a directory full of free themes and you simply select what suits your niche. The "Feature Filter" helps you find what you require. It looks like this:

Once you find what is most suitable for your blog, click install, and you are good to go. It takes about five minutes for the new theme to be installed. You follow the same steps to install a paid theme from ThemeForest.

Another option to install the right theme is via dashboard. It can be either free or paid theme. Start by downloading the theme from the directory. Like this:

The downloading is easy. Then move to Appearance>Themes and click on the Add New icon like this:

Click on the *Upload Theme* icon and move to the **Choose File** icon and then browse through the themes and click *Install.*

If the uploading is complete, you will option to activate, live preview and return to theme page. You should click activate and theme installation is complete.

Page VS Post

Beginners in WordPress confuse pages and posts. This free

platform has two content types by default pages and posts. What is the difference between pages and posts?

- o Pages are not timed, and posts are timed

- o Pages are not social while posts are.

- o Pages are usually hierarchical while posts are categorized

- o Pages cannot be included in RSS feed while posts are included.

- o Pages have their custom feature while posts do not

Tags, Ranking, and SEO

What are Tags and How to use Them in the Correct Way?

Tags help you group your posts with similar details. When a visitor clicks on the tag, WordPress opens the tag page and indexes all posts with the same specific tag. Tags help to keep your content organized and have a huge impact on SEO. Tags are basically how to make your contents visible.

The Importance of Search Engine Optimization on Page (SEO on Page)

How does Google work?

Google is an authority over all other search engines available. Over time, users get more value from Google search engine as it has invested in the best automated programs to ensure users get the information they need almost instantly. Delivering relevant results at any given time has been a plus.

That said, a smart blogger would want to know how Google works in order to position oneself. The primary goal here is the consumer. Google is available so that consumers get answers to all their queries and concerns. Google is out there to fetch the best results and deliver to a client. As a blogger, you are very secondary to Google. Google will prioritize you if you will in turn give the most value to Google consumers. Therefore, it is important to know that your content must be of top-notch quality and sufficiently meets consumers' needs on the web. If you are the most satisfying provider, it goes without saying; Google will rank you so highly that you will be on the first and top page of Google's search engine results page (SERP).

Google works with mathematical algorithms to filter through their database and deliver the most relevant of results to end users. They have not publicly stated what the algorithms are, and it is squarely in order so they remain anonymous since for one, they are in business and letting out why their search results are almost perfect would only be sharing company tactics and strategies with competitors. Secondly, publicizing the algorithms will not guarantee safety to users as rogue bloggers will have a chance to cheat the system. Over time, only smart and hardworking bloggers have learned how it works up the ladder. Those working right have seen their efforts bear fruit.

How Google Ranks Sites in 2019: Top Ranking Factors

The above is an all-time favorite question to any blogger who means business. It is important for one to have the understanding of Google's pagerank in mind in order to get the best out of the effort put to release quality content. Search Engine Optimization SEO is the lifeline.

Besides the fact that the top-ranking factors are anonymous to bloggers from Google, the following proven tactics have identified some factors to be true and proven to work. You cannot just fail consider them. It will be the difference between your success and failure.

Having in mind that 97% of Google users only look at the first page of the results and never bother to click on the next page, this is how to win a spot on the first page and possibly the top three organic results:

Content Quality

"Content is king" is not a cliché in blogging, rather, it is the motto. After all is said and done, the foundation of writing and having a viable presence online is quality content. Every other factor builds on this. You are already a success if you have mastered the art of juicy content. It all starts here and that is what will primarily drive people to your blog. We can't emphasize the importance of quality content enough; it is great that content quality leads to the other winning factor of quality backlinks.

Quality Backlinks

You must be an authority in your niche for another website to consider having you on their page. It means you have to have been of great value to them and they cannot do without a link to your resource. The many links to your page by other pages is a credible voting system for Google top ranking factors. The more backlinks you have, the more credible Google finds you.

While we are at it, do not forget the word quality. Having every Tom, Dick, and Harry backlinking you is not a smart move. Therefore, seek authority websites to link back to you, as the former might be more detrimental to your blog. Be wise and carefully check out those who want to collaborate with you.

Though we will discuss more about social media and blogging later on in future chapters, it is important to highlight at this point that your content going viral on social media and the inbound traffic to your page, is something that catches Google's eye. They are in the end always ranking your site on the quality backlinks when people choose to share your content.

Secured Sites (A shift from HTTP to HTTPS)

Google is out to protect her users from hackers and other people with ill-motives. They want to ensure that when a client is browsing through your website that all their information is kept safe from intruders. Having security in your blog will mean you mean well for your clients and it makes it a common goal for you and Google. Secure your sites if they indeed matter to you. Google will surely reward this effort.

Page speed

We live in fast times. Consumers want their results either now or now. Your page should take up utmost 2 seconds to load up. Anything other than that will see people moving fast to sites which seem to consider the value of time in this day and age. There is so much to do with so little time, so whether someone is online for work or for social reasons, you will be surprised how both do not have a second to waste.

Work on your page speed. Google in an effort to satisfy their clients, will give priority to sites with great page speed.

Webpage Content Length

After a long time of working to optimize web pages, we have learned that lengthy content wins the top ranks. We would want to assume the more you offer, the higher the chances of a client getting all they need on one stop. This is not in any way a call to have you stretching your content from East to Waste losing your focus and gist. In most scenarios, brief is sufficient. Jump in with both feet and through all lengths, short and long, in your site, watch and learn what works for you and your niche.

Mobile friendly Websites

Many websites only considered desktop user experience from the word go and as was pointed out in our WordPress section, that is a big mistake. Mobile Devices are the easiest and most accessible tool at any given time. If you even realize half your audience is on the desktop while the other half is on their phone, it is only smart to be on both service points. The fact that almost everyone has a smartphone, means that once in a while they will be doing their searches on phone. Anytime a client visits a site on mobile and it is not friendly, almost all leave for a better experience. Why would Google risk it to prioritize you?

Domain age

Whether or not the age of a domain is anything to judge its credibility on is debatable. However, the age of a site can be judged by Google or any search engine on its viability. There are too many new bloggers who do not last, so being patient and focusing on why you started in the first place is critical. Being around for a while and offering consistent and quality content from the beginning will set you up as a better authority figure.

Google Updates and How to survive them

Google updates are responsible for the most severe fears that bloggers tend to have. Why? Because you might be ranking high or appear on the first page consistently for several years and then your ranking falls due to some changes in algorithm. If and when there are Google updates, this is how to survive them.

The above points we covered on Top ranking factors still hold true, so continue to use best practices in utilizing them. In other words, be proactive and continue to update them periodically (remember trends change, so stay on the top of the wave). For example, keywords are big to garner top rankings but how and when to use them is paramount to know. Today voice search is a big deal and it is obvious that Google is big on it too. Factoring the voice search engine on your site is non-negotiable now and in the near future. It could be a top reason as to why your rank is falling after an update.

Do not be hasty. You cannot diagnose the changes with Google updates at face value. It will call for time and a great deal of auditing and reflection on your site. It is also beneficial to contract experts to do the audit for you. Once updates are out, many sources run to explain the why and the how, but few are legit. It will take seasoned digital marketers and the Google team itself to get to the truth. Be careful not to follow masses blindly and instead let all your effort count and be timely while at it.

The competition for an audience and great conversions online is great. Google updates are bound to happen to cut out the fake and manipulative participants, as well to move people from comfort zones. Remember, your top slot is sought after by many and you are only king or queen of the mountain, as long as you can hold it. Every day, you have to earn your rank.

Perfecting on good SEO skills and being in the good graces of Google (and by extension the other search engines) is a daily struggle for all content creators. Brace up for perfection and being the best always! Here are my suggestions for the most powerful SEO Strategies that you can implement from the start.

Authority

The qualitative measure that sees to it you are visible and ranking at the top is authority. You are an authority with quality content and quality links to your site. Page authority will have your site ranked higher while domain authority will also push you to the top with your popularity and age of domain.

Trust

Just like with human interactions, a site has to build an online presence that is trustworthy. Google will only rank your site if they trust you to be legit and competent with your content. Social media will go a long way in pushing for backlinks as this also makes your site trustworthy. You acquire trust when many people want to associate with your site.

Relevance

You become relevant the moment your content commands attention enough to attract backlinks. When Google ranks every backlink, it creates citation flow. They only consider backlinks from sites considered as trustworthy, thus creating a trust flow.

How to Structure your Blog for Easy and Automatic SEO

The above points will be effective if we structure our content well. The following steps show how to structure your blog for easy and automatic SEO:

Shift from using as many keywords as possible and focus on 1-2 quality long tails keywords. The rule is always clear, you are required to sound natural and not sound like you are trying to force keywords. Flow and naturally placed keywords especially with question-based long tail keywords will most likely excite your visitors and make it easy for conversions to take place.

Images are good for your blog post as they reinforce your message. However, you have to optimize images as well by putting the right caption, introducing the image with a good description, and having a short explanation of the image. Now that search engines cannot see an image as we see them, the well-intentioned texts will do the trick.

Avoid Duplicating Content and Giving Searchers What They Want

Be careful with duplicating content for the simple reason that in most cases, it is not usually a duplicated content literally, but using similar tags that can make search engines mistake them for duplicate content. Therefore, making visitors confuse your content for another person's or literally going to the wrong site.

Some ways to prevent this type of confusion is to use a URL structure guide for visitors and making sure that at every point of your site the URL matches the topic or the subtopic you positioned for the particular that link. It helps visitors have an easy time navigating your site. In most cases, they can simply change what they want to read by clicking a key work on the URL. For example, one can click the word 'contact' to 'home' and easily switch from the contact page to the home page.

The next tip is to maximize on the opportunity of using internal links. When writing about one topic in your blog page, it may require a brief intro from another relevant topic you had written on earlier and published on the same blog. You will not only sound repetitive to return visitors on your site by writing content again, but you will be limiting yourself from creating new material. Instead, create sub links that would naturally link back to all other pages you deem necessary for the current page content. This will allow your visitors to choose the topics they wish to review, instead of re-reading past information.

Another suggestion is to go big on Google analytics and trends. Let me explain, many times it is easier for an entrepreneur to solve an existing problem by creating a solution. When you visit Google's console you realize that most people have interests in a particular topic, why not jump in early enough and provide the much needed information?

A bold title with the main keyword will help the reader know whether the post is relevant to their search or not. Keywords in H1 and H2 headers also go a long way in ranking pages. Google will also rank it if it deems it important to the search question at hand. A great blog with not only good content, but with visible, clear titles and subtitles will help a reader have an easy time from point A of the communication process to point Z. Subtitles show a writer who has organized thoughts and points. It makes it easier even for a reader who is short on time or one looking for something specific on the same topic to skim through fast and successfully.

The Importance of the Sitemap

A sitemap is one of the greatest tools to employ for SEO. Submitting an XML Sitemap to Google is not a direct ticket to being indexed as Google is primarily out to crawl your content and rank it. A sitemap will require you to be consistent with your content in line with the issued side map for the following two reasons:

Usability

A visitor should have an out of this world user experience when they visit your site and click the links that you have provided. There should be good flow of information and page speeds should be as fast as possible. Also, your site should be clean and easy to view.

Responsive

A visitor wants a responsive website, whether it is you responding, an administrator, or an auto response, the visitor should be responded to as quickly as possible. When this is primarily factored in by the blogger, then one easily increases their website value.

The Importance of Link Building: Why is linking building so important?

Link building (as we discussed earlier about building credible collabs) is the ultimate process of creating partners online and branding your online presence as it is the only way web pages link to each other. It is critical to build your page links as this makes you an authority according to Google. As well, when someone links you in their page, they are basically inviting their audience to visit your page. In most cases, they direct visitors to you as an expert and one who has something they probably would not do without.

Paying to get Link on Website with Authority

Would you be willing to buy advertising space on that blog? Or would you be willing to pay to write a guest posts on the authoritative site? The two options will see you paying to be featured there. And the visibility is guaranteed. Also, the fact that you want to associate your blog with the ones already setting pace in the market is a great effort on your part.

Paying to get a link to a website with authority is considered as an unethical practice by Google. If you are caught, then the consequences will be dire on your site. Now that backlinks are a crucial part to ranking your site,

Google expects a fair ground for all participants.

The greatest question is, why would you prefer shortcuts? We believe the process in every product or brand ultimately makes the whole difference. A genuine blogger would take the long route at least to prove to oneself you deserve the victory that will be preceded by sweat and strategy. You may pay your way to the top and then realize you cannot sustain yourself up there, yet you already lost money paying for the site.

The only way to pay for backlinks from authoritative sites is to pay with your outstanding content. You will agree with me that it is costly to bring out a brainy and smart piece of a read, but use it as needed or as you see fit.

How to Acquire Links and What to Avoid in Link Building

When you become an expert in your niche, you will be offering unmatched content online that others would want to associate with and create leverage on. Naturally, you will attract link building networks your way or have collaboration opportunities with other large influencers in your niche. In the next chapter, we will look at different ways to monetize a successful blog.

Chapter 3: Other Monetization Methods Part 1

Affiliate Marketing

You need to position your blog or website with quality products and services to draw more visitors for greater visibility. The hope is that these product producers and service providers will notice you as you are already standing out with your content. Reach out to your friends, partners, and family to have you on their web pages. Networking will go a long way here to improve your legitimacy and help you monetize your site. The first step in using product and service partnerships to grow your revenue and site traffic is to establish good anchor text. The anchor text points to the product or service links as a backlink. A web page will require an anchor text that is a hyperlink to redirect a visitor to the intended page (of the product or service) with either more information, illustration, or a place to purchase the marketed product or service. You will be compensated by either commission or a cut of the sale price of every sale you generate. More detail is below.

1. What is affiliate Marketing and How does it work?

Affiliate marketing is one of those golden opportunities bloggers have found to make money easily and with little real effort. Imagine yourself as a seasoned blogger with millions of readers per month having been given a product to recommend and refer your audience to the brand owner. In return they give you commissions or cuts of the sale for the conversions from your blog. This is the epitome of the of the term passive income. Affiliate marketing tops the ways an influencer can make money while they sleep.

It is the greatest wish for most bloggers, to wake up one morning and just look at the rising zeros in their bank account. All for placing a link and sending your readers to the brand owner or the service provider. Then as they buy the product or sign up for the service, you earn money for directing traffic and new customers to that particular business.

Affiliate marketing only requires you to identify a company or a business owner whose products you can comfortably recommend in your blog. They just seem a natural fit for your niche. For example, a travel blogger can easily recommend the top and best hotels in a particular area, or a nutrition blogger may recommend meal delivery services. When people use your referral link to book spaces in the hotel or sign up for a month of meal kit delivery, you get a commission.

In most cases there are multiple influencers or affiliates on the web competing to market the service or the product. This is the network that enables the whole process to work as it usually results in a great deal of sales for the business. The influencers that send the company the most sales are retained, while the others are usually cut loose. The top sellers or affiliates are given bonuses and discounts for their readers. This usually results in more sales for both the influencer and branded company.

This is how bloggers or influencers use the system of

affiliate marketing to push the products of the business owner. It is these factors that motivate brand owners, knowing that he or she has a sales force of affiliate marketing that earn no salary and are only paid when they produce. The networker will ensure the process is smooth as possible by placing clear referral links their customers will see and will work hard to promote the product, as they get paid to do that.

Now I am going to take you through the journey of becoming an affiliate marketer. I'm going to give you the step to step guide to pick the best products or services for your niche. Even before you start your blog you are probably choosing a niche by keeping in mind what product you will wish to promote. These are the products that will sell easily, or you know you will be able to promote with little effort. So naturally, you will have to find a product that will flow smoothly with your content.

Explore the different affiliate programs that are available and brainstorm the one you would like to pick (or more-you are not limited to just one affiliate partner). We will look at the 10 most popular and most rewarding, then you can be in a position to pick the best. You will even be in a position to explore more from the knowledge that you'll pick up. We are also going to look at the strategies and tactics employed to make your affiliate marketing efforts as natural as your blog. This natural appearance to your audience will encourage more clients to convert to sales by recommending you and the product to others. Here are some reasons why anyone working as a blogger or social media influencer should become an affiliate marketer.

Controlled Competition- Even if we sell the same

product as many others, the likelihood of you being put out of business by them is low. The normal scramble for market share is eliminated, as your entire business is not tied up in selling the product or service. Also, your marketing is based on your niche of interest and not the product. The product is simply an extra you offer to your readers, not a requirement. If they choose to buy it, it is because of the value they think they will get from it. Your ability to draw customers or brands is not based on sales, but on the amount of traffic you get to your site. Even if that is unpaid traffic. So, all others promoting the product are on equal footing, except for their traffic numbers. The clients who like your communication techniques and audience numbers will ask you to promote their products no matter how many others they have already partnered with.

Boundaries do Not Apply- A company in the USA will not hesitate to reach out to an influencer that lives in Europe or China as they probably draw an international audience. The American company (or international company) will be anxious to provide the product to a population that may have never heard of it except from the influencer. You sharing with your local and a worldwide audience makes you valuable to them. The product or service you researched and found on your affiliate program will help the company in the USA and yourself, as an affiliate marketer, make sales that would otherwise have been impossible.

Built in Audience- The above points lead us to the ultimate challenge, how to continue to build your audience and seek to maximize the most benefit from them. Once they have all bought the product, then how do you continue to build sales? There are only two ways, partner with another product (new to your audience) or seek new followers. The latter is most beneficial as you do not want to be accused of churning (or bleeding your audience for sales). That could lead to your loss of followers as you are seen to be just a salesperson, not someone giving them useful information. It is best to partner a long time with one or two companies that add value to your audience. That unique value will help continue to earn you subscribers and help the passive income through affiliate marketing to grow.

Most Popular Affiliate Programs

Loosely defined, an affiliate program is a set of systems or network that enables the process of affiliate marketing to be easy and smooth. It is the intermediate program between companies and affiliate marketers. You can imagine a company like Amazon or Loot Crate can have over a million affiliate marketers across the world. The programs are simple and cheaper than the internal employment and sales system, with its payroll, sales tracking, and the taxes that go along with it. Commissions are universal and much easier to account for and credit to the affiliate marketer. The product is drop shipped or the service is provided through established means, which is much easier where logistics are concerned.

Below are the 10 most popular affiliate programs that bloggers with good followings (and some without) can make some money with.

1. ShareASale Affiliates

ShareASale is one of the oldest affiliate marketing websites in the world. It has a heritage and it is known to have even digital paying options aside from the normal standard payment options that almost every other affiliate website has. It is a bit more complex than other programs. ShareASale affiliates does not necessarily require great technical know-how; it's just that it's a bit hard for beginners to figure their way around it. Commissions vary by promoted products.

2. Amazon Associates

Amazon is by far the biggest of the affiliate programs and is the most popular with influencers because there is no limit to the products you can offer and they give up to 10% commissions of the total sale. When I say total sales, unlike other affiliate programs that vary commissions by products, there are always at least 20 items on amazon where you earn a solid 10% on the sales total (minus tax). The other items have varied rates from 5 to 7%. They also give you credit for sales made through one of your links even if the customer doesn't buy the product attached to the link, but purchases something else. This happens when they click your product link, but stay on the site to do further shopping and purchase other items. Amazon has varied payment options, thus making it convenient. Also, you can market and sell your own products from Amazon and keep all the profits minus shipping. This can be passive or not, as you will have to either create, list, and ship the product or ship a bulk amount to an Amazon Warehouse to ship for you for a fee as they are ordered. The fees can be built into the selling prices if you can still keep the prices competitive.

3. eBay

We find this to be a favorite for online influencers, because you can find anything and everything under the sun on eBay. This gives most bloggers flexibility and a choice on which product they wish to market and refer their clients. You can also market and sell your own products from eBay and keep all the profits minus shipping. This is not quite passive, as you will have to create, list, and then ship the product. But it can be much more profitable than partnering with an eBay seller to market their products. You can also employ a dropshipper for an additional fee (which you can build into the selling prices) to take a lot of the work off your shoulders. Some popular dropshippers are below and you can find their sites with a simple search.

1. Doba – #1 Drop Shipping Company

2. Oberlo – Marketplace for eCommerce Products

3. Dropship Direct– Wholesale Drop Shipping

4. Sunrise Wholesale – Wholesale Dropshipper

5. Wholesale 2B – Best Drop Shipping Wholesalers

6. SaleHoo – Dropship Wholesalers.

If you choose to partner with a seller on the site (rather than market your own product) then commissions are split between you, the affiliate marketer, and the eBay platform. This can be much less profitable than getting commissions directly from the brand company. However, it is still additional income that with enough volume can yield profit.

Note if you choose to use to partner with an affiliate partner that utilizes an auction to sell an item, then there is a possibility you could receive less or no commission. For example, if it takes more than 10 days to close the sale or if the item sells for less than the suggested retail price, then you will lose on all the commission's you had acquired on that particular auction. It is a well known glitch and we highly advise not using auctions but direct sales on all products that are not directly sold by you.

4. Shopify

For direct sellers you can earn subscription fees for the first two months you start working with them. To top that, you earn as much as $598 on their standard plans. You also have a 100% share of their enterprise plan. There is a lot of money here that may inspire partners to offer higher commissions to their influencers. Like eBay and Amazon, Shopify offers both affiliate marketing and direct sales with varied payment options.

5. Bluehost Affiliate Program

For a blogger who is doing a niche that addresses other upcoming bloggers who would need a site, or entrepreneurs who are yet to create or own a website, this referral rewards may be for you. The pay or commission is limited to the rate you can convert your followers website owners via Bluehost. Bluehost is currently one of the top recommended WordPress hosts available. With affordable prices, flexible packages and a great customer support team, there's a convincing argument as to why they're so highly recommended. Maybe it's time you partnered with them too and gave your followers a value for their future sites.

Choosing products or a price range for affiliate products

If you go about your business or spend a lot of time shopping, the one thing you will notice is that the products on sale are either very expensive and only a few pieces get sold per month, or very cheap product that sell really fast so when the former sells say 100 pieces the latter sells 10000 pieces.

In Affiliate marketing, high ticket affiliate marketing sees to it that an affiliate marketer sells on average very expensive products and the conversions from the referrals usually come back with high commission compared to the total amount of revenues the company gets. Consequently, you will find an affiliate marketer struggling to make commissions with low ticket affiliate marketing which involves products that are very cheap versus an ebook is going for $50. The marketer may sell less of the ebook, but those carry much higher commissions than a cheaper $10 item, so in the end, quality may outweigh quantity.

So, choose high ticket affiliate marketing because you do not have to sell huge amounts to make decent money. This is very beneficial if you have a smaller following that has disposable income or just a smaller following in general. Whereas, if you have a larger following then a lower ticket might work as well. The best thing is to make the most out of an opportunity and vary the items or services you promote. Another thing, people are more likely to shop for expensive products online nowadays, because online is often where you get the lowest price relative to the product or service. Shopping online sees to it that at least one gets a chance to compare prices and get the most out of something. Shoppers will check for the best price and the best reviews on items or services.

Blogging is not just a game. It is an industry just like any other. All the necessary work ethics that will propel a company to the top, make the highest of profit, and command the largest share of the marketplace are the same efforts and factors needed for a successful blogging career. There is no single business where one can just pick a random product without having a clear understanding of the market, the needs, the problem, and the solution that will bring revenue to the solution provider.

So bearing that in mind, why would a blogger just pick a niche for the sake of it without having the end goal in mind? From this guide you will get to know all the facts and expectations in the field of blogging so that when you start off you are equipped. If today you were to go on a road trip into some interior region the wisest thing to do is get a rough idea of the distance you will cover so that you budget for enough fuel to and from your destination.

It pains me to see the number of projects and businesses people pour money and effort into only for the projects and businesses to be left hanging and undone. It is a waste of resources. Why would you even waste your time studying all these materials we provide and others only for you to start a blog and pour your heart and content into it only for you to get tired in the middle and never even get to monetize or earn money from it. We have highlighted the above scenario so that we get to the serious part of blogging. Yes, you need to select a niche and at the back of your mind you need also to be clear and have plans on what products you will engage with in your affiliate marketing processes. The following are the best pointers to selecting the niche of your blog first looking at the best products on the programs:

What is available on your affiliate marketing program- Do not pick a product that is not related to your niche or that no one else in your niche is providing. A nutrition blogger would not necessarily offer a traditional processed cake mix, while a baking blogger might. A product has to be there in your niche, You have to check on its features and how fast it is selling, and you have to check what it will be worth to your followers.

Now that we have talked about high- and low-ticket affiliate marketing strategies, pick your side. Will you rather sell a few affiliate products and get high commission, or will you go for products that are cheap in value and move fast? The most important thing is, among all the available products, what will you be most comfortable offering to your followers and incorporating into your content? Finally, does the value in commissions matter to you? If yes, go for the highest of figures that will motivate you to be creative and think and work on your blog around the clock without getting bored. After all, money should be enough motivation for effort and hardwork, even if you are tired.

Your strength and the opportunity to train from the best- My growing pursuit for knowledge is motivated by the person I am becoming each day. Mental and intellectual growth is fulfilling and making me want to share it with others. You will continue to work hard, and your blog will thrive. The many clients that I have gotten the opportunity to serve are more than grateful and have benefited from the information I provide. So make sure any brands you partner with fits in with your brand and bring that benefit to your followers. Never compromise your morals or reputation to make a quick dollar, if you choose carefully people will buy the product to get its benefit. Your job will be easy in the terms of sales.

Have a heart for leadership by serving -Lead naturally and with the idea of serving those you lead. Strive to see a team of people using the resources at their disposal efficiently. Your work ethic and work delivery has to be excellent and exceptional. with the goal of educating your audience. Choose brands/companies that mirror your objectives. Make sure they mirror the leadership through service model by having a quality/useful product/service and having hands on customer experience. If the brand mirrors your own, then you should feel confident in partnering with them and leading your followers to them.

Stay passionate about research and learning- Your writing stays up to date with world research and top business trends that affect your niche. You constantly read, watch videos, and keep informed about the latest information that your followers will need to effectively participate in the niche. Your knowledge is why people seek out the advice of a professional blogger and ensure your blog's success in the future. Make sure your partner brands also keep up with those same trends and constantly improve their products.

You provide a wealth of network relationships-

After months or years of producing a quality blog you build a network of other niche influencers or entrepreneurs. that operate in the niche. You will keep abreast of what they are doing and promoting. You should use that as a way of discerning between brands. I am affiliated with various blogs and organizations that are quite resourceful. I use those relationships for the purposes of learning, networking, sharpening my wits, and giving back to society. Being influential in an industry is a huge responsibility that should never be taken lightly. Association with any brand means you will make it visible to a greater audience than just yours.

The World is a Village- The internet has made the world a village. You have to take time to study and understand people. You have to be very multicultural thanks to current global economy. Make sure to appreciate all people and try to serve everyone from every walk of life by giving the best information possible. Personally, I had an encounter with a handicapped blogger who was making over 20 million USD annually and that changed my life. The encounter left me better and excited about life. From that one session, I purposed in my heart to serve society through it. My mission in life is to see people have the best online experience possible for them to fill fulfilled in life. Make sure both your niche and affiliated products hold up that standard.

You should always be grateful for the opportunity to present yourself to a potential global audience. Write well always, you never know who is reading. A potential client would be in your blog reading, see something that inspires them, and then later pour a lot of money in your endeavors. Always write for this kind of client. Focus on not disappointing them but exciting them then later getting the best from them no matter where in the world they are.

Choose a few related products-services for cross and down sell-Excellence is the act of making the most out of available limited resources. As a blogger, you wear the heart of a salesperson and teacher. Once someone visits your site and the client becomes convertible, it is your duty to ensure that the client is in a shopping mood. Make sure you not only sell the item the client came for, but you suggest more products related to what the client is buying - this is called cross selling. If at any point the client falls back due to cost constraints, you take the opportunity to downsell and sell cheaper available substitutes.

The above case scenario will only play out successfully if you as an affiliate had already done your homework. The homework is picking a product that you will use for your affiliate marketing and understanding all the other related products that you can sell to a potential client. Have other products available that are of the same value in terms of content, information, satisfaction, need solving capacity, but for a cheaper price so that you'll be in a position to sell either way. In short, choose products and services that are related to your core product or service in a range of prices.

How to pick up the products-services that sell the most

The following is the smartest strategy to employ when seeking to find the products and services that sell the most through affiliate marketing. Do your research. You can know what product is selling fast in the market by watching trends and sales on larger retail websites or on the brand sites. The best-selling product and the best service companies in the world are what you should focus on. Search for it and pick what will interest your readers and move fast and consistently. You will never go wrong with either fast-moving consumer goods or home appliances that we use every day, or we need to replace often.

Packaging your blog with ebooks that offer more value is one of the shortest ways of identifying what moves fast. This is because people are in your blog already seeking information concerning the niche you are in so offer more on that at a price. Most importantly visit those blog sites that are doing well and are even being published in successful magazines or as top companies in the world. Check out what they're selling to earn big commissions and follow suit. Follow the money.

How to be the best-selling affiliate-Many people have had their paths cross with rogue and unqualified "professionals" and the results can be devastating to say the least. I had a friend that had an unpleasant experience with this type of "expert." As a young adult, my friend and his sister were mistaken for some troublemakers near my high school and were arrested for trespassing at a Subway restaurant. His parents hired a lawyer that was affordable at the time, but unfortunately the results were disastrous. The attorney was not fit for the job and the case concluded with a plea bargain. I remember the judge asking the attorney if he knew what he was doing. I am certain that if my friend had a competent defense, he wouldn't have suffered the agonizing experience of clearing up his reputation after it was over. Imagine how many lives are affected because of incompetent legal representation. Thereafter, a strong passion and desire was birthed in my friend. He decided that whatever field he choose he would be excellent. This motivation makes me question anyone who just lives life just for the sake of financial benefit only. Don't be an example of a singular money chaser.

You should aspire to want to change people's experiences online. Why would you refer your loyal readers to a product that yourself would not spend money on? It has to be different and it has got to start with you. Be industrious and open-minded. Believe that success is a sweet gift to be enjoyed by everyone regardless of status and race. And is paramount when it comes to people spending their money on genuine products.

You need to have hands on experience on entrepreneurship, branding, sales and marketing. This are things you are supposed to acquire from the general school life. A cousin of mine first launched himself in the music industry by playing local media houses with his twin brother. It was smooth, fun, but not as profitable as expected. He took a sales job to make ends meet and in the middle of his music career, he grew successful in sales and quickly grew over the ranks as a salesman at one of the largest cruising companies, Norwegian Cruise Line.

He was able to successfully grow a sales resume working for various companies which finally lead him to create a travel agency, Executive Roadside & Travel. He decided to go into business for himself and quit the sales job to operate his roadside and travel business. Through consistency and focus, he was able to sustain a modest income and attract the attention of my roadside service provider, National Motor Club. In less than a month, he ran the fastest growing division and took home the coveted award of divisional manager of the month during his first month. At the moment, he is now running a travel blog that has is popular for the information offer travelers and allowing them to purchase services/products needed on the road. Yes, it wasn't his original plan, but he made a great passive income and is able to travel to pursue his music as well. So if life gives you lemons make lemonade; it is just as sweet, even if it wasn't your first flavor of choice.

Using affiliate links in the most natural way as possible-No one in the world wants to feel sold. Remember a bloggers primary task is to provide quality content that informs. When you compromise your good content for sales then you deserve to be left by your readers. This is because the principal stands, people over profit. Why can't you first serve the needs of the people who are visiting your blog and after you have satisfied them go ahead and lead them into your sale strategies? It is not wrong to sell but when you sell just to sell you are breaching the contract of why those people visited your blog in the first place.

That said, there is a need to include affiliate links naturally into your content. That is the very reason we firstly recommended that you pick a niche and a product that will work together naturally. For example, if you're still working on a travel company it will be very hard for you to recommend a product like kitchen gadgets. That is better placed in a blog or website about cooking or nutrition. But, a gas discount card or roadside assistance plan would fit naturally in a travel blog. When you use affiliate links naturally people will be more motivated to checkout your offers because the leads to the offers will be smooth.

Giving quality contents before affiliate links (create captivating and interesting contents)

Giving quality content before affiliate links is just going back to your roots of good writing and information. Bloggers are primarily known as people who provide good content concerning the different desires of the public. Affiliate links are simply secondary introductions to a blogger finding a way to earn while serving the needs of the people. It goes without saying, if one prioritizes affiliate links over good and quality content then you are as good as done in the business of blogging. You won't stay long. Put your house in order and prioritize first things first. In most cases, if you do what is expected of you to be successful then success will follow in its path.

Chapter 4: Other Monetization Methods 2

Direct Email Marketing

Gone are the days where bloggers were easily countable around the globe and they would just request readers to send them their email. After a steady rise of bloggers in the market, there have been a series of smart ways identified of getting the emails from clients without directly asking. This enables for you to not only let them know about new content, but to market products and services for pay. This is a great way to make sales without littering your site with links or ads (we will cover this a bit later). Also, it is a great way to keep your name on your readers' minds by staying in their inbox. However, most people will not just give you their email address, so we have to use alternate methods to get them. Here are some of the best I have found.

Lead magnets are the strategies that bait readers on a blog with a worthwhile product to have them send the email so that the product is in turn sent to them via email. Lead magnets require you to go a notch higher and know for sure what exactly you would need to offer visitors and get the desired response. The following steps will surely make your efforts bear fruit:

1. Conduct research and get to know what is that one thing that people would love to have in their emails and make a difference in the lives of businesses. The best way to the answer is to ask. You can start with the smallest of email contacts you already have and can also use your social media to ask friends

and followers what do we want most to get from you for free. It is good to know also that following up on your platforms comments from people who follow you religiously with questions will be a good place to start because simply you'll be giving them what they have already requested from you. Existing followers will be happy that at least you listen to them. This will be a plus on your reputation

2. You also have to be outstanding, because as a reader yourself you know a reader can never have enough on the shelf to read. Even when the available written material would take a million lifetimes to accomplish. We are always enticed by new material. Because we are more inclined to the now and the future, so make sure your material and content is enticing.

The Importance of Email Marketing: create lists and advertise related products

Since the email mode of communication has become mainstream, email marketing has always been a classic way of doing top notch and targeted marketing. When a client gives you his email or subscribes to your emails it means they are attracted to your keywords and blog placement. So they are more likely to read and respond to your email messages. The following are key thoughts to remember when creating an email list and advertising related products there.

1. An email is a direct message to a particular recipient who had proven to be on the same niche with you and is interested in your particular

keywords.

2. When sending an email to such specific audiences is more likely to create more conversions to your advertising materials that are sending their way.

3. Online, Comparison, or direct shopping is a trend for many people and getting an email with a suggestion of potential items one can buy is a great opportunity for many.

4. The email should provide direct links to products on sale, so the process of conversion is easy and you do not get to lose a potential client who postponed to go and check a site later because they were not really available. This happens when one is seeing an ad anywhere else but, on their computer, or phone.

Most email lists will be gathered from your blog directly, or through emails sent from your blogs to those requesting information or to those referred by other visitors. However, you are limited to only your direct traffic. There are many other ways to both attract others to your site or generate sales off your site.

Creating an email list outside your blog.

Make use of sites, like forums, that are outside of your blog. You should be a regular contributor or poster on free open forums that discuss your niche. This is a great way to leave links to your blog, email list, or products. Many people Google a niche and start on a public discussion forum rather than an individual blog. But, that doesn't mean you can't be on the forum as a fellow discusser. This will show people your expertise and they will seek you out.

An effective placed link will bring them right to you and your email list.

Also, social media is a great place to start. You can use both your pages or accounts or a forum/group. You can place links or advice on the forum or group (as long as the admin allows it). This will be a post by post type of strategy. Another way, especially on Facebook is to pay them to advertise your lead magnets. This a process known as social media targeting and it is an effective way to generate email leads. You can choose to run advertisement on Facebook (or other platforms- we will discuss how it works later in this guide) and pay to reach people (based on interests, location, or personal factors) to get your free lead magnets. The ad or promotion will only reach those persons who will be interested in what you are selling or the information you are offering. All of them will be of the mindset of "I want to be part of what you discuss in your blog" indirectly. In other words, you are more guaranteed an audience of your choice on social media, than any other platform. You ask why? This is because this is where everyone is spending their time on. You will find potential clients on Facebook, Instagram, YouTube, and Twitter enjoying their social time.

Secondly, now that you are running a blog on the internet, you are bound to get more conversions if you advertise on social media than on any other media platform. No One really watches traditional TV or listens to radio anymore. There are limited opportunities for leads on streaming services and online radio, but they are expensive. There is no better way to get people clicking on your lead magnets than creating catchy captions on Facebook and putting the headline of the lead magnet in bold. I guarantee that you are more likely to get instant visits to your site if you advertise it on social media as the lead to your blog is only a click away. This is a far better option than advertising on television or radio and someone needing to go either on phone or PC to look out for you.

Facebook can tailor your ad to reach the right audience for you. You only reach who you want to reach and pay for just that. While running your adventure blog, you might want to write about hiking events at a site of your choice. If you live in Dallas, most probably you know people in your community who love travel and you will want to advertise to them while promoting local tourism. As well, the fact you will be writing about them is enough for them to give you clicks. Also, depending on your content, you can, go beyond targeting a particular location, even going as far as pinpointing what mile radius your town of choice should reach. You can specify gender, age, hobbies and interests of your target audience. Here, you get more value for your money. Go ahead and target that audience from anywhere in the world that you feel are likely to be interested in what you offer and in turn, their emails will make a difference in your traffic and sales.

With social media, you are sure to create an email list faster than you would in any other way. You not only have to advertise on social media but be active there and interact with potential follower and fellow influencers. You could also pay or strike collab deals with other bloggers outside your niche to advertise/shoutout you in their space. In this case, you will tab into a more diverse audience that may not have the same interests but may have a need you can fill.

What should your email send include?

Most subscribers to your blog visit it regularly, so what should you include in your weekly emails? Take that golden opportunity to send your new posts directly to them along with partners or affiliates that easily relate to those posts. You might also want to send special posts (not available on your normal blog) to your subscribers. This will be an inducement to remain on your email list and give them a feeling of being in an elite class of follower. Do not just push sale only emails to your subscribers. Just remember generally if you do this, most of them will either unsubscribe or mark you as spam.

Keeping Subscribers engaged

It doesn't matter to the world what you do to make ends meet or if you are making money from your blogs, all people want is to get their needs met. Are you capable of meeting them at their point of need? Yes, you can only do that by offering the best of content and information. If you are then you will keep the quality content coming and anyone will be to continue reading your blog or opening your emails. Blogging has no age limit. You can blog as young, old or in between and get the same opportunity to make yourself great! Would you be willing to take that risk and do whatever it takes to make it at the top?

This point reminds me that blogging welcomes everyone from every field in life. Whatever interests you or whatever lessons you have learned in this life can be shared with others for you to make a decent income in return. Blogging will give you the chance to awaken all your dreams. Which may have either been buried because of lack of money or lack of a flexible time that would allow you time to pursue your dream. Imagine you can your use laptop and work from anywhere in the world! Imagine being a travel blogger and actually traveling to blog or a pet care blogger than fosters animals and documents that experience. This should be motivation to find ways to make as much great content as you can and live the best life on your terms.

Blogging embraces everyone no matter what their situation is. In fact being "different" can be an advantage while blogging, as most people want to read about a life unlike their own. People can write about life in a wheelchair, having physical impairments, or other limitations that may seem difficult and inspire others. While certain disabilities my not work (easily) in other industries blogging and writing good content is all inclusive. It will require you to dive in with everything you are. It is known that the best writers, artists, and comedians have proven to have operated from their worst point of sorrow, but still empowered others. Some have been depressed to the edge of suicide and actually left us with masterpieces of their genius brains. They proved to the world that despite life being how it is, they were willing to excel in their craft. No betrayal, no pain, no fear, should make you hold back your writing talents. Write your pieces every day like they are your last or a measure for a Nobel peace prize or some other international award!

Can you write unapologetically well? Can you give your all without trying to fix your imagination to fit our usual confines of society? Let people read your work and experience life in totality. Readers sharing in your deepest joys and your wildest dreams. Write and let them walk into your life every time you publish yourself and leave them longing to read and live your life again. The only limitations of writing are the ones in your head, and they are not real.

Remember that Google (and other search engines) have set standards and they are on the radar to check if your content is great and helpful to their users. Therefore, you must be trustworthy and do what needs to be done to stand and be counted as a top blogger. With the above in consideration every day, why should you fail to deliver content. Write to impress, and give your best shot each round. Make sure this comes through in not only your blog, but in the marketing emails you send.

Chapter 5: Other Monetization Methods 3

Advertising on your Blogs

Blogging and media work for money is the agenda here. You create a mass of audience by giving them information they need, education, entertainment, or a combination of all these items. You lay out your life for them to see so their minds and emotions are refreshed. In turn, the audience you gather behind you can be used to create income or generate money. This process is called monetization and so far, we have talked about affiliate marketing and email marketing and sales. Affiliate marketing and Email Marketing are both great as seen above, but it is not the only monetization process. There are many ways to generate an income using a blog as the anchor. The information below is an overview to the world of Direct Blog monetization.

As a blogger, you have worked hard to build a loyal audience and fanbase for your blog, as well building a readership with thousands of readers daily. For example, your travel blog is having 3000 visitors a day and that pet care blog is generating daily traffic of 5000. These are a good number to start converting to money. How do you do it?

You can place ads directly on your blog. As your visitors read your postings, there can be strategic adverts in the site, usually appearing on the sidebar of the site, but they can pop up over the text. Therefore, be careful about the types of ads you use on your blog, as you do not want to drive readers away. You can either sell that space directly or link your page with Google AdSense that will channel ads to your site. The two styles will be discussed later in depth.

As an authority, you can write recommendations and reviews of products and services and receive money from the mentions (affiliate links). But some useful products may not have affiliate programs or not allow sites like Amazon to make them part of theirs. So, using straight up ads are the only way to integrate those products into your blog. The best products and services to advertise are the ones directly connected or related to your niche. In this case if you are a travel blogger, you can do recommendations of hotels, airlines, tours and travel companies, tourist attractions sites and cities, unique wear and fashion from the different areas you cover. The Pet Care blogger can advertise pet food, pet accessories, adoption, foster, or rescue programs. You are already trustworthy and respected enough to be an authority, so be careful when choosing those products. Below is an overview of the types of ads that are regularly on blogs.

All of the following methods and types of ads have two avenues of achievement. The first and most profitable is to be your own agent and broker by negotiating with companies and other bloggers for advertising on your site. This takes a lot of work up front, but once done, it becomes a very passive way of making money. The second is to partner with either Google AdSense or AdWords (Google, Reddit, and YouTube), Facebook/Instagram, or Twitter for targeted ad placement on your site or Social Media for money or for targeting advertising of your site, blog, products or services to increase your audience and sales. It is definitely a circle of life, so to speak. In an upcoming chapter we will look at all these methods.

Types of Ads and Methods of Using Them

Publishing Contextual Ads

Contextual advertising connotes the word context. Context involves keywords. This is a smart way for a client to pay for a specific targeted audience to get their ads. A blogger is also guaranteed more ad clicks with the right audience landing the related ads. Here, search engines are smart to channel advertisement where the context displayed matches the industry of the product or service. Search engines are also in a position to categorize and reach the intended users of the contextual messages.

The best example for Contextual ads is Google's AdSense. This is how Google knows what traffic they can channel a particular ad for maximum click on the ads. The ads also can be URL specific If you choose to skip AdSense and sell your space directly to companies, they usually have a similar system using search engines to do the same thing.

As a blogger, you are paid by impressions (the number of times and ad is viewed, it is measured by the pause and reading of it. Click through Impressions are the number of times someone clicks on the ad and visit the advertisers page) any additional can go in your blog. The advertiser pays for each Click Through Rate (CTR), and it can be profitable, so consider publishing contextual ads only. However, remember you must not overwhelm your readers with ads, so the make sure all ads are of the most related product or service to your niche or blog.

Using text link ads

As the title suggests, this is an ad placed as text in the normal context of your writing, but then it is highlighted and hyperlinked (very similar to you placing affiliate links yourself). A reader who wishes to click on the ad may either be redirected to a new page with the host advertiser or the blog may redirect him to the advertiser on the same page. For a reader who was no interest in the ad, the redirections may make him lose interest with your blog and you may lose the reader. Many a times, they are too annoyed to return, so make sure to make wise choices or make sure these ads are easy to spot for those who do not wish to click them.

Yes you are selling to people, but you should not make anyone feel sold. That's the name of the game. In-text ads usually have the advertiser pay a blogger pay-per-click. This is the most common, but sometimes a blogger may be paid a flat rate fee for advertising in their blog. It is purely negotiated by you up front with individual companies or outlined in the Terms of Service on Google AdSense.

Placing Impression Ads

Companies can also pay to place impression ads that appear when people are searching a particular niche or pay you for the same status when people search a term on your blog. You can also pay to advertise your blog to others using the same system. Placing ads impressions work with two factors; placements and keywords. You can use either of the two or combine the two to get outstanding refined results. You have the power to decide if you wish your ads to be featured on all selected Display Networks (the sidebar of the Google search page where the ads remain static and never change, since the advertiser has paid to be there whenever the keywords are searched) and you also decide the budget to go into the same, whether you are paying or being paid.

When you use both factors to zero in on your audience, you enjoy having refined audiences who are likely to click on your ads and convert with great sales. You also are in a position to earn more as a blogger if the two factors are applied. Placements make it easy for you to play with your bidding chances for higher wins on your end as an advertiser. Placement can also help you to place bids on the exact URLS of your taste.

In addition, you can pick keywords and direct ads to websites which only focus on the industry you are in. You are better placed when you are in control of who sees your ads. What you pay as an advertiser for clicks will eventually convert to sales or traffic (to draw more paying advertisers) with reasonable rates.

Publishing Sponsored Reviews and Paid Posts

An advertiser may choose to write a very good review on his product or service then approach you to publish it on your blog. Or, they may even pay you as a blogger to write and publish a review on the product on your blog. This is direct advertising and it pays well since there are no intermediaries. However, this is an ethically gray area as you do not want to endorse a product or write essentially an unfounded review on a product or service, you have not used. Proceed with caution and make sure you give the product or service a whirl and be honest in your endorsement.

Advertisers can shy away from doing a direct review of his product and prefer some mentions and endorsement on a post. The post might be talking about touring Mt. Kenya while the blogger chooses to focus also on the accommodation he had at the client's hotel. The blogger ends up selling both Mt. Kenya as a tourist site and the client's hotel as the best choice while at it. Just make sure you have actually stayed at the hotel.

Guest Posts

Guest posts are the shortest route for a blogger to make their brand or blog known to other readers in another influential blog. For beginners and newbies, guest posts will skyrocket you to greatness. Here you tell people, "hey, I have not been around for long, actually I just started blogging, yet I am so resourceful you should check me out". If the guest post is likeable and informative to them, then you will easily win yourself followers. In some cases, you will pay the bigger blogger for the chance to guest write for them and in turn once established smaller bloggers and influencers will pay you to do the same.

Guest posts benefit your blog in three ways:

1. You earn from someone by simply taking the time and writing for your blog.

2. You earn time off your weekly schedules because your loyal readers will find something to read that is informative, while you took some time to rest from your schedule or get ahead on your posts for later.

3. You prove to your readers that you are influential enough to attract guests to your blog. This helps seal your value and makes you a leader in your niche.

Placing your own Ads selling your Products-services

Oh, this is beautiful, and it is my favorite. This is where you reap the fruits of your efforts. Imagine having a blog with a monthly traffic of 2 million readers and going ahead to run a business that will directly benefit your audience! It sounds fun. So sometimes it will become necessary to pay for ads to sell the product or service you offer. Personally, why I choose to endorse this mode of advertising more, is because of the rule of reciprocity. Today if my favorite blogger decides to sell some jewelry or perfumes, I would definitely want to promote them. Even if as a way to say thank you for keeping me on my toes for their next publication.

Loyal readers are more likely to promote your business if they see it outside your blog. This can be either as a legitimate business person, product inventor, or being advertised as an expert. If they see paid promotions from other influencers or ads on Google, then it established your validity a more than a blogger. This will make them feel more at ease in promoting you and they will share your content or product/service. You may be out 200 dollars in paid ads, but you may get 500 dollars in sales and free advertising through shares and shout outs, because of the perception of being legit.

Now what can you sell? I mean the possibilities are limitless, but make sure whatever it is it relates to your niche and blog in a natural and fluid way. If there is not an existing product you can sell, then create your own. The most obvious is putting a very detailed and expanded niche advice or information into an ebook. You are already a writer, so why not write manual or informative book, beyond your blog? Being a published author carries a huge amount of weight, especially if your niche and blog are mainly information that would not easily tie to any other physical product. Your business does not have to involve anything else other than writing or it can be an actual product, service, or gadget. Just find something valuable to sell. You will do well, especially if you have created an audience for yourself already. It is only fair you do yourself some a favor and take advantage of the ready market. Why create influence to help every other person sale their products yet deny yourself the benefits?

Don't be worried about how to get your product out there. In the case of a book you can self-publish through Amazon Kindle or Audible, as well as many other sites. Then you market it to your built-in audience and possibly others.

Remember we are going for 500 hundred people giving you 20 bucks a month to reach 10k a month. This is just another way to hit that average. So, no book deal is required. Though that is a possibility, you can write a chapter or two and send (along with complete information on your brand, blog and reach) to an existing publisher. They may have the systems in place for marketing beyond your means, and they may offer you money upfront and a cut of sales to put it out or buy it outright. The possibilities are endless, just make sure you crunch the numbers and do what is most profitable.

In the case of a product or gadget, there are many companies (just Google ghost or 2nd party manufacturing) that will work with you on developing things like skin care, cosmetics, supplements and gadgets to your specifications and produce them under your brand. Just make sure once you know what you want you put together the blueprint or formula and get a patent, so the idea is yours. There are many websites like LegalZoom that can help you file for a government patent if it is needed. There are fees involved, but to start your own business, it is worth it. The same is true of a service. Put together a game plan and perhaps offer it free or discounted to a few people to get good reviews. Then market it to your audience.

Displaying Ads in your Blog's Feed

There are many companies will pay you to channel traffic to their site at a fee. A good example is Google's AdSense. You will need to sign up for an account with them and give your full details including payment ones. On your WordPress website, assuming you are using WordPress, click on the WordPress widget, then click on appearance, then select widgets, pick custom HTML and drag it to the best location on your site then drop it there. Remember to paste the Google AdSense code. From this point, you will be golden, waiting for advertising money to reflect in your bank account.

With Google AdSense, you do not have to worry about finding individual advertisers yourself. Although you will have to part with half of the ad revenue due to Google AdSense pay model. This is simply because you did not broker your own deal with the advertiser, but Google did. Google acts as a middle man and brings advertisers to your site for a cut of the fee. This brings us to our last option for now. Read on.

Selling Ad Space Directly

You can have such a great blog that advertisers will be either be approaching you directly to feature ads on your site or responding when you reach out to them about a deal. So you will find yourself booking sales meetings with potential clients to sell them advertising space. Whether you go fetching for them or they come, the bottom line is you have advertising space up for grabs. Here, you make a lot of money and you pocket it all.

Apart from writing great content, selling as space should be another priority. It pays well. Have fun selling it. Just note somewhere, you will have the added job of finding and brokering deals with clients, along with managing and creating for your huge visitor traffic to your blog or site. Let traffic building motivate you to increase the worth of your advertising space. Again, just like other forms of advertising, make sure you are choosing relevant and helpful companies to partner with.

Chapter 6: Using Google and Social Media for Profit

In this chapter we will explore the uses of both Google AdSense and Google AdWords for both getting paid advertisers on your site and social media, as well as advertising to grow your own audience. We will also cover the basics of using the various forms of Social Media to grow your brand and advertise.

Google AdSense

To first get started you must create a Google Account, this is as simple as creating a Gmail account. Go to Google to do this. This is what will allow you to use the service, which is an advertising brokerage site. Basically, companies pay Google to place their ads on busy or related sites that will cause people to click on their ads and buy products.

Companies trust Google and their algorithm to do their best for them. Google has reach and reputation that you and I do not have, so partnering with them is a great way to go for generating ad revenue.

To create your AdSense account, follow these steps:

1. Visit Google AdSense

2. Click Sign up now.

3. Enter the URL of your website or blog that you want to show ads on. This could include both a YouTube Channel and Reddit Account. You can also set this

up directly through YouTube (Google owns YouTube) and then it will link to AdSense.

4. Enter your email address.

5. Click Save and continue.

6. Sign in to your Google Account.

7. Select your country or territory.

8. Review and accept the AdSense Terms and Conditions.

9. Click Create account.

You are done.

For most sites the approval is pretty easy, especially for WordPress, which is a reason we suggested it. Smaller sites like Wix may have some issues, but as long as the site is written in a basic HTML manner it should be fine. For all sites (except YouTube-which requires 4k watch hours in a one-year period and 1k subscribers to qualify) you do not have to have a certain threshold of traffic, but it helps to speed up the process. Bear in mind that you must reach Ad Revenue balance of at least 100 dollars to be paid, so if you have a small amount of traffic, it may take a while to get paid. Once the account is approved, you will tell google about your niche and demographic, so they can choose appropriate advertisers.

Google AdWords

Different from AdSense, AdWords is a way for you to advertise your blog, site, product, or service to others by being placed on relevant sites and pages. Just like you are paid by clicks and impression in AdSense, you pay by them on AdWords. Think of you being one of the companies that is paying to be on your site, but instead you are paying to be on someone else's. You trust Google to place you based on what you tell them about your site. Basically, it is the polar opposite of AdSense. To apply you go to AdSense and fill out an application, and you will be contacted. Rates and programs very, so the application must be done first.

Using Social Media

In this chapter we will learn how to harness the power of the various social media sites to both promote your blog and generate sales. Social media should be a passion and a hobby for everyone who wants to succeed in the online world. In the media industry, it has been being called "the new media" and is replacing traditional sources of news and information at a rapid pace. It is a phenomenon in the market that is still new despite a decade having passed since it is emergence. Researchers are studying it day and night as it has proven to be impactful, fast, and phenomenal in the hands of one who knows how to use it. Social media has changed the rules of the game completely. It has combined the powerful social world with the economic part of it and the results are fireworks!

For the first time in history, a brand has an opportunity to create an audience around it without using mainstream media for publicity. The latter was expensive and remained a luxury for the rich. Today, social media is so affordable, yet you can have the same and more rewards one used to get in the past through mainstream media after paying a fortune for a few seconds in front of an audience. People spend so much time on social media that you can get a lot of time in front of a targeted audience, instead of a mass random audience.

How wonderful that you can create an online presence that can spark emotions as intended, attract likes for instant endorsement and reactions, openly invite people across the globe to comment and debate around the issues you have raised openly and instantly, and attract people to share your message to their circles. The last point requires some time, but it is what every blogger should dream of. In social media, when almost everyone seems to share your post or video, the shared content is referred to as one "going viral".

Remember the audience we said earlier that you now have power to create? Yes. That audience takes time to grow. With good effort and great content, you can grow it into millions of followers. When you share content, most likely it is visible to the community you have created around yourself, in this case, your audience. When someone decides to share your work, it means they have taken a deliberate decision to share your content to their circles and audience. It is the best thing; if you have 2 million followers, you are only guaranteed that many people accessing your work. But when say 10 people with 2 million followers each shares your work to their circles, then we are talking of up to 22 million people seeing your work! Isn't that impressive! Google will take note of your impact and definitely rank you at the top. You are now an influencer and your work will be pushed more for more to see.

Social media has the potential to build your brand. A brand requires creation of awareness to a potentially large amount of people. The more the people know your brand, the better your position to your competitors. There are no shortcuts here. If you are good and have great content, the results can be quick. The masses will like you, celebrate you, and share you. If your work is below average, then you will go unnoticed or even be ridiculed for years. It is a great platform to help sharpen your teeth but be sure you share only accurate or useful information. Progress and growth will attract a steady flow of people looking at your content and recommending it to others.

Social media is relatively cheap compared to all other media. Yes, you will have to work with a budget, but at the end of the day, it is thousands less than any other media channel. The mind-blowing fact is, you spend less, for even more guaranteed conversions and impact! Google appreciates and recognizes backlinks from social media. They will rank you higher from your effort there. Ultimately, you will be on top of the SERP (search engine results page) if you crack social media success with you blog!

The above are reasons that would make anyone want to jump in social media with both feet! But, below we are going to discuss the nitty gritty details of how to launch yourself on this massive platform. The fact that almost 80% of the world's population is on social media and almost 50% are active users should ring success bells to you.

We are going to learn the step-by-step guide to launching and running social media platforms. Last but not least, we will look into how to achieve success in all platforms, creating harmony.

Create a profile on the main social Networks

Blogging takes a leap higher when launched on social media and we are going to zero in on the major platforms; Facebook, Instagram, Twitter, YouTube, Patreon, Reddit, and Quora. All are social media platforms, but they work differently to achieve more or less the same goal. Below is a roadmap to each of them.

Facebook

Facebook is undoubtedly the most popular of all social media platforms. Actually, most people think the term social media and the term Facebook are one and the same. 2018 statistics showed that despite having over 4 billion registered accounts, it has an impressive 2.27 billion active users! This is massive!

How it works

Facebook allows you to create a profile as a person or business. You will have your profile and cover photo to put a face or any identity you may wish with your name. It allows you to share as much about yourself as possible. Your location, education history, contacts, family members, hobbies and interests, books and movies you have read and watched respectively, your favorite pages, your public groups on the same platform. You can answer random social questions your friends might be interested in, places you have visited, and so much more. Basically, others can live your life with you.

In addition to the above, Facebook allows you to have up 5000 "connects" referred here as friends. Beyond 5000, all others who wish to link up with you automatically become your followers. Here, you can have as many numbers of followers as you possibly can.

On the business side of the platform, Facebook prompts users to "share what is on their minds". Here people will create content and write about anything and everything. One can write content and/or back it up with an image, a video, or a shared link to a blog post. Basically, you can write content, share captivating images or informative illustrations, share videos, and best of all for you, share your blog posts with your audience/friends.

Facebook will give you an opportunity to create a page independent of your personal account, if you wish. You can run your page as a brand name based off your personal name. You can be either an independent publisher of your blog or the face of your blog if you work as a team. In most cases, it is more rewarding to work with the brand name of your blog. Remember, you are here to build a brand for your blog. A page will allow you to specify your niche and give a brief description of your blog. For example, if you run a travel blog, you will indicate travel as your main agenda. You will also go ahead and describe the extent of your adventure and content. This way, you will attract an audience that is interested with the same things as your blog. You will realize you will attract a lot of travel enthusiasts and all other matters related to travel.

Below is a step-by-step guide to winning on Facebook with a page already in place

Make clear your intention. Unless you are a news blog, more often than not, you will want to confine yourself to a niche. Remember news is a niche on its own. What is my point? Be a master of one niche. Let people know what niche you specialize in. Be a resource for good content on one particular area of life and create Audience on it. This will see to it you create a steadily growing number of Audience who are likely to stay loyal to the blog. You don't want to attract someone because of travel matters only for you to jump ropes and start engaging on totally different matters like religion and politics. In most cases, this will be a put off to the people who followed you for travel. In the end, you will have very unpredictable followership as people come and go.

Rarely will anyone invent a wheel in this day and age. That said, there are many people running blogs like you do and doing the same niche as you even on Facebook. How do you stand out? Your competitor may have 10 million followers. You can equally match him and have 10 million followers. It is possible to run a page that has hundreds of millions of followers while your competitors have tens of millions of followers. We all know what is great stands out. These are not figures you fantasize about and they appear. You work for them and your content will have to be top notch.

Accompany most of your shared blog posts with captivating captions. Bait Facebook users to want to read more. You are more likely to get clicks on your blog with either a very catchy caption or a very catchy headline. If you have both you have massive chances already.

You cannot open a page to only share blog posts. Wrong move. You will have to do other independent things to create a life and presence on your page. Actually, if you run a page that only shares blog posts, you are more likely to lose big time. I believe in the thumb rule of reciprocity in the universe. Choose either to be informative, educative, or entertaining. Let people follow you for the above. You will keep them coming. Then once in a while, share your blog posts, and as a rule of thumb, people will want to reciprocate your good effort in their lives for the above three and promote your blog. Or, if not for that reason, they will always be curious if your blog post is a greater version of the value they get from your other offerings.

Marketing and Advertising on Facebook

Any brand worth its name today has advertised to get there. Advertising is the process by which you pay a media channel to push you to their mass audience. Say Facebook has a potential of 5 billion people on their site. You pay them to reach that number of audiences. But if you pay to reach 5 billion people, you will have to cough a few more thousand dollars unlike one who will want to pay for only 20000 people, consisting of only women, age 28-35, located in say, California only. You realize the latter cluster of Audience will achieve more for less. This is what you get when you pay Facebook to advertise your blog.

Today if you advertise yourself on a daily newspaper, you are sure that your target audience will be localized, since daily news in USA cannot really sell in Japan. While on Facebook there is a guarantee of more audience on social media than on dailies. What we are trying to say is you are more guaranteed of an Audience of your choice online, and on social media, than any other platform.

Secondly, now that you are running a blog on the internet, you are bound to get more conversions if you advertise online than on any other media. Say you own The Washington Post, you are more likely to get instant visits to your site if you advertise for it online as the lead to blog is only a click away, rather than advertising on television, requiring someone to go either on their phone or PC to look out for you.

Facebook can tailor make the right audience for you. You only reach who you want to reach and pay for just that. While running your blog, you might want to write about hiking events at the second tallest mountain in the world, Mt. Kenya. This is a global destination. If you live in Texas, most probably you know there are people in your state that love travel. Most likely, you will want to advertise to them and at least advertise to Kenya, the hosting country while promoting local tourism. As well, the fact you will be writing about them is enough for them to give you clicks. Also, depending on your content, you can go; beyond targeting a particular location. You can even go as far as pinpointing what mile radius your town of choice should be, or you can specify gender, age, hobbies, and interests of your target audience. Here, you get more value for your money.

Instagram

Instagram is popular and has a specific kind of audience. Here, images are everything. Images precede captions. If you miss it on imaging, most likely no one will bother with your great caption. We are talking of 1 billion monthly active users. For a brand that depends on people and viewership, this number is mouthwatering, and you would want to make the most out of it. Instagram was purchased by Facebook last year, so the same targeting opportunities are possible.

Remember our travel blogger. What is travelling without pictures? You are more likely to thrive on Instagram than on any other platform. Besides great content, photography skills are needed here. Whether you perfect the art of photography, or you pay an expert to do it, or you buy images online, the choices are many and all are great. Do what you may, to win an audience with simply good photography. I cannot emphasize this point enough. Photography is king here. Instagram should motivate you to also win at photography even in your blog posts. A blog is beautiful with a picture here and there. For a travel blog, pictures could be enough for a blog. You might need only minimum captioning. Pictures should be unique and high quality, do not just post downloads or screenshots. Make Instagram the album of your life.

On Instagram, the same rules on marketing and advertising applies as they do on Facebook. It gets better since they are under the same umbrella company. You can cross-advertise the same item on both Facebook and Instagram. How wonderful! You know, you might want to target Texas audiences only, just that, and you might find a very active user on Instagram who does not either own a Facebook account or has one but hardly checks in there. To get this person, you will have to advertise on both platforms to be sure of getting as much attention to both Facebook and Instagram lovers.

Twitter

Twitter is uniquely different. It doesn't have as many users as with the other two mentioned platforms, but twitter followers tend to be very loyal to twitter. We are talking about around 326 million daily active users. Twitter is the debate center of the world. People who are more into intellect and conversations over images and social fun. Your captivating blog posts will do well here. People are most likely to read and follow links here. This is because they are inclined to seek out more information and evidence for the discourse they have been following here throughout the day.

You can easily make yourself an authority in blog matters here. Besides sharing your blogs and interesting tweets here and there, the biggest task on Twitter is to follow conversations. Engaging on developing and current topics on trending hashtags is more likely to make you visible than creating just content in your own space.

Engaging someone on twitter will most likely invite them to want to know more about you, and if and when they visit, find you specializing in an area of their interest, then they are likely to stick with you for life. First by following you. Twitter will also give you an opportunity to advertise and feature your ads on their platform. It is a very effective tool for anyone who is keen to invite new readers to their space.

YouTube

YouTube is the second largest search engine in the world, reaching 10 billion people daily. As you probably know, it is video based, so you will have to adapt your strategy a bit here. Instead of just sharing things relevant to your blog in the form of posts or pictures, here you will need to adapt your blog for audio/visual audiences. Videos are a great way to market yourself as people get to actually see and hear you. Also, the interaction on YouTube, as well as the opportunity for the AdSense money is second only to Google Search. In addition to AdSense, there are several Google Partners which we will list below that can market your channel videos on third party sites. YouTube can really help gain you a following.

Making video content of your blogs (VLOG) or content related to your blog is the best option for YouTube. You can link your blog, place affiliate/sales links, or links to your other social media in the videos or video descriptions. It is a chance to provide another type of content for your followers and engage with them. In addition, you will get a whole new audience that does more listening or watching, than reading. Not because they are lazy, but they are busy or just prefer to hear and see their information. Your followers who find you there will also be able to see and hear you, which gives your blog a whole other dimension.

Also, YouTube is a way to get extra ad revenue from AdSense by allowing Google to place ads on your videos (once you have 1k subscribers and 4k watch hours). Furthermore, you can advertise through AdWords to get your videos in front of a targeted audience, thus increasing traffic to all your sites. In addition to AdSense there are some other services (Google Partners) that can market your YouTube content and blog for a small fee. This list is courtesy of <u>Google</u>. Some of them are:

Product Name - *Company Name*	Vendor Type
A9 *A9.com, Inc., Amazon Europe Core SARL*	Vast Provider
ADTECH GmbH *Oath*	Vast Provider
ATK Media GmbH *ATK Media GmbH*	Ad Server Advertiser
Action Allocator *Explido Webmarketing GmbH*	Research - Analytics
Ad VRF (Compete Pixel Study) *Compete, Inc*	Research - Analytics
AdAction *Delta Projects AB*	Vast Provider
AdAction *Delta Projects AB*	Vast Provider
AdGear Technologies Inc. *AdGear Technologies Inc.*	Vast Provider

AdMotion USA Inc. *Admotion USA Inc.*	Vast Provider
AdTraxx *Explido Webmarketing GmbH*	Research - Analytics
AdVentori SAS *AdVentori SAS*	Vast Provider
Adap.tv Inc. (AdWords/YouTube) *Oath*	Vast Provider
Adform *ADFORM A/S*	Ad Server Advertiser
Adfox *Adfox*	Vast Provider

Adition *Virtual Minds*	Vast Provider
Adloox *Adloox SA*	Research - Analytics
Adluxe *HyperAdvertising Ltd*	Vast Provider, Ad Server Advertiser

Admetrics GmbH	Vast Provider
Admetrics GmbH	
Adobe Scene 7	Creative Agency CDN
Adobe Systems Inc	
Adometry by Google	Research - Analytics
Google, Inc.	
Adrime	Vast Provider
Weborama SA	
Adssets AB	Ad Server Advertiser
Adssets AB	
Advertising Technologies LTD	Demand Side Platform
Advertising Technologies LTD	
Alphonso	Research - Analytics
Alphonso	
Aperture	Research - Analytics
PulsePoint, Inc.	
AppNexus Open AdStream	Vast Provider
AppNexus Inc	

AppNexus AdStream *AppNexus Inc*	Open	Vast Provider
AthenaHealth *athenahealth, Inc*		Ad Server Advertiser
Augur *Augur Technologies Inc*	Research - Analytics	
Barometric *Barometric, Inc.*	Ad Server Advertiser	
Bluestreak *BlueStreak*	Ad Server Advertiser	
BridgeTrack *Publicis Media GmbH*	Vast Provider	
Campaign Monitor (YouTube) *Integral Ad Science, Inc*	Research - Verification	
Celtra Inc. *Celtra Inc.*	Vast Provider	

Channel Intelligence *Google, Inc.*	Research - Analytics
Cheq.ai *CHEQ AI Technologies Ltd.*	Vast Provider
ClickTicker, LTD *ClickTicker, LTD*	Ad Server Advertiser
Clinch.co *Clinch Labs LTD*	Ad Server Advertiser
Collabo LLC *Renegade Internet, Inc*	Ad Server Advertiser
ComScore (AdXpose) *comScore Inc.*	Research - Verification
ComScore vCE (YouTube) *comScore Inc.*	Research - Verification
DEVK *DEVK*	Research - Analytics
DeltaX *AdBox Software Pvt Ltd.*	Ad Server Ad Network, Vast Provider

DoubleClick Bid Manager *Google, Inc.*	Demand Side Platform
DoubleClick Campaign Manager *Google, Inc.*	Ad Server Advertiser, Vast Provider
DoubleClick for Publishers Premium *Google, Inc.*	Vast Provider, Ad Server Advertiser
DoubleVerify Inc. *DoubleVerify Inc.*	Advertising Option Icon
DoubleVerify Inc. *DoubleVerify Inc.*	Research - Verification
DoubleVerify Inc. (BrandShield): Ad Swapping *DoubleVerify Inc.*	Ad Blocker
Duepuntozero Research SRL *DUEPUNTOZERO RESEARCH SRL*	Research - Brand Lift
DynAdmic Corp. *DynAdmic*	Ad Server Ad Network

Corporation

E-Plus Mobilfunk GmbH & Co. KG *E-Plus Mobilfunk GmbH & Co. KG*	Ad Server Advertiser
EUROZEST MEDIA LIMITED/Avid Ad Server *EUROZEST MEDIA LIMITED/Avid Ad Server*	Ad Server Advertiser
Extreme Reach Digital (ER Digital) *Extreme Reach, Inc.*	Vast Provider, Research - Brand Lift
Extreme Reach, Inc. *Extreme Reach, Inc.*	Vast Provider
EyeReturn Marketing *Eyereturn Marketing Inc.*	Vast Provider
Eyewonder Inc. *Sizmek Inc.*	Ad Server Advertiser, Vast Provider
Flashtalking	Vast Provider

Flashtalking, Inc.	
Flite Inc.	Vast Provider
Flite Inc.	
FreeWheel	Vast Provider
FreeWheel	
Gigya	Ad Server Advertiser
Gigya	
GoldSpot Media	Ad Server Advertiser
GoldSpot Media Inc	
Google Zoo	Research - Analytics
Google, Inc.	
HLEB	Ad Server Advertiser
Blueworks Commerce Inc.	
HRB Digital LLC.	Ad Server Advertiser
TruEffect	
Hindustan Times Mobile Solutions Limited	Vast Provider
Hindustan Times Mobile Solutions	

Limited

IBM Experience One (Unica)	Research - Analytics
IBM	
Ignite Technologies	Research - Analytics
Ignite Technologies, Inc.	
Innovid Inc.	Vast Provider
Innovid Inc.	
Insight Express (AdIndex)	Research - Brand Lift
Kantar	
Insight Express (Mobile Ignite)	Research - Brand Lift
Kantar	
Internet Billboard, a. s	Ad Server Advertiser
Internet BillBoard a.s.	
Jivox Corporation	Vast Provider
Jivox Corporation	
Kreditech Holding SSL GmbH	Research - Analytics

Ingenious Technologies	
KuaiziTech	Ad Server Ad Network
KuaiziTech	
Leadcapital	Ad Server Advertiser
Leadcapital Corp	
Liverail Inc.	Vast Provider
Facebook, Inc.	
Local Marketing Institute LLC	Ad Server Advertiser
Renegade Internet, Inc	
MASSMOTIONMEDIA SARL	Vast Provider
MASSMOTIONMEDIA SARL	
Mashero GmbH - VAST	Vast Provider
Mashero GmbH	
MeMo2 / Hottraffic	Research - Brand Lift
Hottraffic BV	
Metro Parent	Ad Server Advertiser

Renegade Internet, Inc

Miaozhen Systems	Vast Provider
Beijing Miaozhen Information Consulting Co., Ltd.	
Mixpo Inc.	Vast Provider
Netsertive, Inc.	
Moat Inc.	Research - Analytics
Oracle Data Cloud	
Monsoon Ads Pvt. Ltd.	Research - Analytics
Monsoon Global Ventures Inc.	
NET-Metrix-Audit	Research - Analytics
NET-Metrix AG - Switzerland	
Nextperf	Vast Provider
Rakuten, Inc.	
Nielsen (Brand Effect Extended View [BEEV])	Research - Brand Lift
Nielsen	

Nielsen (Sales Effect)	Research - Analytics
Nielsen	
Nielsen (Watch Effect/Net Effect)	Research - Analytics
Nielsen	
Nielsen Digital Ad Ratings	Research - Analytics
Nielsen	
OOO GPM-Digital	Vast Provider
OOO GPM-Digital	
Omnibus co. Ltd.	Data Management Platform
Omnibus co. ltd.	
OpenX Ad Server	Vast Provider
OpenX	
OpenX OnRamp	Ad Server Advertiser
OpenX	
Platform IQ	Vast Provider
Platform IQ	
Pointroll	Vast Provider
Pointroll	

Proquire LLC - Accenture	Research - Analytics
Proquire LLC - Accenture	
Rakuten Attribution	Research - Analytics
Rakuten, Inc.	
Reamp	Ad Server Advertiser
Comune SA	
Reddion	Research - Analytics
GroupM	
Renegade Internet Inc.	Ad Server Advertiser
Renegade Internet, Inc	
Republic Project, Inc.	Ad Server Advertiser
Sizmek Inc.	
Research Horizons LLC dba Phoenix Marketing	Research - Brand Lift
Research Horizons LLC dba Phoenix Marketing	
Research Now (YouTube)	Research - Brand Lift

Research Now Limited	
RevJet LLC.	Vast Provider
RevJet LLC.	
SPACE ADSERVER	Ad Server Advertiser
SPACE TECNOLOGIA E INTELIGÊNCIA LTDA	
Samba.TV	Research - Brand Lift
Free Stream Media Corp.	
Sizmek	Vast Provider
Sizmek Inc.	
Skillup Video Technologies Corporation	Vast Provider
Skillup Video Technologies Corporation	
Smartstream.tv	Vast Provider
SMARTSTREAM.TV GmbH	
SpongeCell, LLC	Vast Provider

Flashtalking, Inc.

SuperAwesome	Ad Server Ad Network
SuperAwesome	
Symphony Advanced Media	Research - Analytics, Research - Brand Lift
Symphony Advanced Media	
TF1 - FR	Research - Analytics
Groupe TF1 S.A	
TUI UK Limited	Vast Provider
Flashtalking, Inc.	
Target.com	Research - Analytics
Target.com a division of Target Corporation	
Telemetry Limited	Vast Provider
Telemetry INC.	
Telogical Systems, LLC	Ad Server Ad Network
Telogical Systems, LLC	
Tender Industries AB	Vast Provider
Tender Industries AB	

Teracent Corporation	Ad Server Advertiser
Google, Inc.	
The Walt Disney	Research - Analytics
The Walt Disney	
Treepodia	Ad Server Advertiser
Treepodia	
Tremor Video	Vast Provider
VideoHub, a division of Tremor Video, Inc.	
TruEffect	Vast Provider, Ad Server Advertiser
TruEffect	
TubeMogul Inc.	Vast Provider
Adobe Systems Inc	
TubeMogul Inc. (AdWords/YouTube)	Vast Provider
Adobe Systems Inc	
Unica an IBM Company	Research - Analytics
Unica	
Unicast	Ad Server Advertiser
Sizmek Inc.	

VideoHub	Research - Analytics
VideoHub, a division of Tremor Video, Inc.	
Videology	Vast Provider
Videology	
Videoplaza	Vast Provider
Videoplaza	
Vindico	Vast Provider
Broadband Enterprises	
Visible Measures Corp.	Research - Analytics
Visible Measures Corp.	
Weborama Campaign Manager	Vast Provider
Weborama SA	
Yahoo!	Research - Analytics
Oath	
YouTube, LLC	CDN Provider
Google, Inc.	
ZEDO Inc.	Vast Provider

ZEDO Inc.	
ZEFR Inc.	Vast Provider
ZEFR Inc.	
b34106183_test	Ad Exchange
b34106183_test	
dbupdate1	Ad Exchange
dbupdate1	
gemiusDirectEffect	Vast Provider
Gemius SA	
iBillboard, a.s.	Vast Provider
Internet BillBoard a.s.	
mov.ad GmbH	Ad Server Advertiser
mov.ad GmbH	
uSwitch	Ad Server Advertiser
uSwitch Limited	

Patreon

Patreon is a social media site that allows followers to "subscribe or pledge" different amounts of money to their favorite influencers. Each influencer creates several levels of support at the site ranging from 1 to as high as they wish. At each level they offer different types of rewards based on the pledge amount. These vary from creator to creator and must be tailored to the things the creator can do consistently. Some examples are private patron only live chats, t-shirts, autographs, exclusive blogs or vlogs posted for patrons to the Patreon site. Basically, just get creative and people can sign up for as little as 1 buck a month. The donations are taken monthly and sent to the influencer.

Reddit & Quora

Reddit and Quora are discussion forums where users discuss and share various types of information. What makes them different is the fact that on those sites users can both upvote information to get more views for it and ask direct questions on various topics. The answers are cataloged and can be shared with others asking those same questions. These are great places to show yourself an authority in your niche and help drive people to your blog for more information. Finally, you can advertise on both platforms using Google AdWords to drive people to your answers over others.

Social Media Strategy

Social media may appear to require a larger work schedule than you anticipated but having weighed all the economic value you get from social media, it is only fair you seriously think and work toward creating leverage on the platforms.

Create weekly or monthly schedules for your special media platforms. You have to have the end in mind. Write down smart goals and objectives. When you start, you have to have goals like, having 1000 followers weekly on each platform. Create themes for each week. With the themes in place, it is very easy to create content around your theme. Prepare images for each content. Set a specific time of day for doing uploads. It can be a morning routine. Say post on Facebook three times a week, then share a blog post weekly if you write your blogs weekly. You can decide to be doing two Instagram posts per week and one link to your blog weekly. You can then have daily twitter uploads and engage conversions there whenever possible. You can make twitter your hobby and go to place to unwind while indirectly creating an impact on your brand.

From the above, it is clear that planning is everything. You do not just wake up and rush to upload items. Then when you are lazy you stay for even a month without updating your pages. Audiences should have some anticipation that their favorite blogger is going to share a blog post every Tuesday 6 a.m. for example. You are the leader here. You set the pace. Whether or not readers keep up, you cannot afford to be the one failing them. The good thing about you being ahead is, as long as the post is up, even if your readers read and engage a week later, the job is done.

Now that you are running the same brand on different social media platforms, it is important to keep a certain sense of identity and personality around you. It is also important to keep it professional and use the same enthusiasm across all platforms. Ok, I realize you may prefer one platform to another, but you have to keep it consistently positive on all of them. This is because the Audience you will get on Facebook will not be the Audience you get on twitter, so you must appear the same on all. Basically, be open and welcoming to all followers.

As well, let the ones you impress on Facebook not be disappointed when they follow you on twitter. One thing, you will have a group of followers who love you so much that they follow you everywhere. With this in mind, you need to keep your A-game anytime anywhere.

One trend that is picking up well on social media is building a following based on controversy. You ought to be careful though what you want to be controversial about. For example, you can be safe being controversial with matters of social ethics, yet put yourself on the line with political controversy. If you are in it for just likes, angry reactions do still add the count of the reactions, commentating, and going viral, but be cautious and pick your battles. Champion something important to those in your niche and try not to rattle too many cages. Let it be just social and not anything that can put you in trouble. Remember, we are blogging for fun and money. However, if you must choose something more controversial than pick a topic that most people can get behind.

A good example would be the problem of society labeling certain people as immoral yet those who engage with them to complete the process are left out of the label. You can post something like this on social media, "The unending debate is a perfect mirrored image of what society is and perceives of power or money. Certain people have a free ticket to doing what they want, when they want, but others are demonized for it. You cannot eat your cake and have it; always being held in higher esteem and allowed to practically do as they wish, while others will be chastised for the same behavior. Such as the difference between sexual mores of men and women, or the legal system for rich vs poor, or the politician class (no matter the parties)." These are issues most people can understand and not get too ruffled over, but other than that, try to avoid controversy. Yes, it is good for social media follows, shares, and reactions, but may not be good for building a blog following.

The above illustration is an example of how to use controversy without being too controversial. By talking about things that most people can get behind you will be riding the fence to a certain extent, which will get people on your page without raging against you. People will share their own perspective and respond to you. Others will tag their friends to come and share their opinions. Such social media practices led to easy fame for many, and it can work for you if you use the right mix of information and light controversy. The primary lesson here is do something out of the ordinary and the comfort of your imagination. You have to get people talking about your blog. The goal is traffic and conversion. Do whatever you what you can, as so long as you do not slander anyone or do not commit any crime. The call here is for you to be proactive. Always be ahead of the pack. You cannot just afford to sit there waiting for other bloggers to set the pace for you. By the time they have employed a creative tactic on their blog, they have already converted the traffic to money and by the time you are copying them, the Audience is already aware of the trick. You want to get them before the practice is common knowledge.

Chapter 7: In Conclusion

Blogging is not a walk in the park, it is a job and can be a rewarding one, but it takes dedication. Please do not enter into the career with expectations of only doing a very light workload for a great living. In truth, it takes many hours of research and writing/rewriting to produce a great blog post that people will read and share. But as well, it is one among the most rewarding ventures out here. Jump in with all you have, dare yourself, and see how much you can pour into a blog and how much great information you can centralize and give to people in a concise manner. It is a system that rewards hard work, dedication, and creative endeavor. But what are some good strategies you can employ from the start to help keep your blog and the information it gives on top of your niche? This will also keep you on the top of the desired sites for advertisers and make sure people think of purchasing your product or service above all others. So, Let's wrap up by looking at some of those.

Staying on top of your niche and popular with advertisers

Growth and progress are key in every field, whether blogging or a traditional job or business. If you start on your own, as your audience grows, so will your needs and possibly theirs. The following are pointers on keeping up on top of your niche and on a good footing with your followers.

You will start to see a lot of messages from your audience that require feedback. This is a side effect of growth and being a good blogger. Remember the customer and follower is king. Keep in mind that even though you have to make a living by converting your audience into money, you know far too well that each one of them matters and you need to keep them happy. This is regardless of whether they purchase things from you or click on ads. You cannot neglect your fan base and that is the measure of your business. When they have simple demands like asking questions concerning your blog posts or having further queries, you will need to answer those question yourself or have a trusted person do it for you. When there are a lot of requests for you to supply more of what you give, such as responding to comments and emails it will cut into your normal writing and social media posting time. This is true especially if you use multiple social media platforms, in addition to your blog. The more places you are will equal more comments and inquiries that cannot and must not be ignored. Doing these tasks will inevitably detract from your normal tasks (the ones that got the blog started). You may be motivated into doing less or shorter researched posts per week, but this is not good for your blog or reputation. So, it may be time to get some help. Just like if you owned a store or cafe, you can't do everything, and a blog is not a small task. Whatever energy you put into creating a superb post to last your audience a week will also be required for daily output and interacting with followers. At this point, you will need a team of support staff or at least a contractor to help with daily tasks. The key here is to carefully choose and train someone or some people who will work to achieve the vision and mission you had in the first place. You need to multiply yourself in others, as you have an intense type of job that starts far before and goes well beyond the creation of a post or article.

You have not just a blog, but a community of peoples, across many platforms that requires your input and direction. I know, "I can't afford help", but you can use websites like Upwork or Fiverr with a multitude of freelancers that work for reasonable prices. Also, you cannot afford to let things fall behind, that will cost far more than the couple hundred dollars per month it takes to hire help. You have to develop a workspace that will churn out work that is needed, but that will not make your audience feel the shift. They have to think it is you answering them and writing your blogs, so to hire carefully is paramount. At the end of the day, the goal is to offer the same great value they come for in your blog in your daily interactions.

Your work and salary now match the many years of creativity and good writing. As the company expands, a team of creatives and general helpers will go a long way in ensuring you keep your edge in the marketplace. You will have to let go of the "I got this" attitude and learn to delegate; this is true of any business that is successful.

That said, in all you do, aim at your original goal of providing great information. Make your every effort count. Make every interaction as creative as possible to give you a good and profitable/fulfilling life. Do not waste it by either a lack of knowledge on how to monetize or for a lack of wisdom on how to navigate the bridge when you get there. The fact that you write well is only the beginning, but your ability to adapt will prove you are capable of earning much. Know that it takes work to translate talent to money. Only a few cracks the code, I think you will be among them. Rise up and take up what you deserve.

I cannot end this book without commenting on the art for art's sake person. I have a great admiration for that worldview, but it can cloud real world realities. Some people only want to blog for the love of writing, but never take into account the money and income possibilities that are available to them from their art. The challenge I pose to the purists is, what is the best way to make money other than from your hobby and passion? In the real world, these kinds of people end up winning more when they learn the art of monetization, even if making money was not their end goal. They can still honor the process of writing well and passionately, but yet get rewarded for it. This will allow them to write for longer and not have to share their time with a "day job". The fact you get paid to do what you love does not discount the art or make it less fulfilling. Quite the opposite, it allows you greater freedom to practice and excel at it. The time you get because you are taking the worry of earning a living will equal greater opportunity to study and get better at your craft. There is no honor in poverty or stretching yourself too thinly, so please let go of that adage.

In conclusion, blogging is a multi-billion industry that is largely untapped. Those already in it have barely scratched the surface. Blogging is the future for most advertising and news/information sourcing. The fact that we are seeing a global downturn in mainstream media sources and more people turning to independent media (blogging is one of these) proves that the market for advertising will continue to rise for bloggers. It is a noble call to invite people to join the profession and tell them for a fact, if they work hard and play smart that it will work out well. Their art and craft will then yield the joys of passive income for now and forever. A life spent doing what you love is the best kind of life.

Resources for Bloggers-as suggested by award-winning Blogger Raelyn Tan. You can find her at her blog

Time Management and Daily Organizing

1. **Evernote**: use it to keep screenshots of my competitor's offerings with the Evernote Web Clipper chrome extension, organize information from market research for future blog post ideas, as a notepad for the things I learn or want to remember, personal organization of my life and more.

2. Momentum: free chrome extension that replaces your new tab page with a personal dashboard featuring a stunning photo backdrop, the time, and your personal to-do list.

3. Mindmeister: Mind Mapping software to create amazing mind maps and organize your mind.

4. Meistertask: Great for getting things done, displays to-dos and projects in a kanban style dashboard which I find really useful.

5. Trello: An alternative to Meistertask.

8. Google Calendar: Free calendar by Google to schedule your time wisely.

9. Focus Booster: Based on the Pomodoro technique, focus booster will empower you to maintain focus and manage distractions.

10. My Hours: Helps you to keep track of where all your

time is going for free.

11. Unroll.me: Easily unsubscribe from multiple mailing lists you are currently subscribed to and go on an email inbox detox today.

12. Sidekick: Sent an email to someone and wonder whether they opened it? Use sidekick and you'll now be notified when the person has opened your email.

13. Dropbox: Free 2gb cloud storage of your files. You can also use Dropbox to store your freebies/ pdfs/ videos and send the link to your readers to access it.

14. Google Analytics: If you aren't using Google Analytics to track your website stats you need to start. The best analytics tool for website owners, hands down. Get data on your website visitors. It's 100% free too! I highly recommend this.

15. Sumome Heatmaps: Because it's fun to see what people are clicking on at your blog.

16. Statcounter: Great for small blogs, as it allows you to see who has visited your website, where they've come from for each and every visitor in chronological order.

Branding, Video Creation & Visual Marketing

17. Screenflow: Highly recommend for every Mac user to use ScreenFlow to record your screen and edit your videos. It is very intuitive and edits videos really nicely

18. Camtasia: Similar to Screenflow, this is a video editing software as well, but for PC users. It is pretty pricey though.

19. <u>Logitech c920</u>: Looking professional on video is a must for me. This makes a world of difference when I'm filming video trainings or holding webinars – from dark and grainy to HD and superb quality! Bonus: When I'm overseas my loved ones get to see me in HD.

20. <u>Blue Yeti Mic</u>: It looks super cool, and the sound quality is awesome! Great mic for entrepreneurs.

21. <u>Lighting Kit</u>: I recommend this lighting kit when filming videos so that your face isn't dark and it looks professional.

22. <u>Canon t3i</u>: My camera which I use to film all videos that do not involve me sitting by my computer.

23. <u>Society 6</u>: Coolass video tapestry backdrops that aren't as ugly as the dreaded green screen

24. <u>Picmonkey</u>: Mad love for creating beautiful graphics for free! Super simple to use too.

25. <u>Canva</u>: Allows you to create beautiful graphics for free too, has nice templates but less flexibility than Picmonkey.

26. <u>VSCO Cam</u>: An amazing free app for editing your Instagram pictures to get a uniform look for your instafeed.

27. <u>Adobe Photoshop</u>: The best tool (and unfortunately the priciest) to create graphics.

28. <u>PDF Escape</u>: Create fillable forms on your PDFs for free.

29. Tinypng: Compress png & jpg pictures without losing picture quality before uploading onto your blog to reduce your site speed.

30. Dimpleart: High-quality caricatures

Writing & Content Creation

31. Coschedule Headline Analyzer: Amazing headline analyzer that tells you if you've a good blog post title or not. Great for writing better headlines!

32. Portent's Content Idea Generator & Tweak Your Biz Content Generator: Ran out of ideas for content creation? These title generators will come up with whacky, amazing titles for your blog posts that will appeal to your audience.

33. Grammarly: Especially great for bloggers whose native language is not English. It finds and corrects grammatical errors, suggest better words for your articles to enhance clarity of your writing and eliminates 250 types of writing mistakes from your blog posts.

34. Open Live Writer: Open Live Writer is a free powerful, lightweight blog editor that allows you to create blog posts, add photos and videos then publish to your website.

35. Getblogo: Powerful desktop publishing tool for Mac.

36. Transcribe: Audio to text transcription service.

SEO & Keyword Research

37. Google Keyword Planner: Nothing like searching

for keywords using the tool created by big G himself.

38. Semrush: The very <u>best SEO tool</u> available. Research on your competitors, do keyword research, and much more.

39. Long Tail Pro: Find Long-tail keywords with this software.

40. Ubersuggest: Google suggestion on steroids – find lots of keyword suggestions for a given keyword!

41. WordPress SEO by Yoast: Best SEO plugin for WordPress users.

Social Scheduling & Autoposters

42.. Buffer, Hootsuite & Edgar: Social scheduling tools to schedule things onto Facebook page/ groups, Twitter and more in advance.

43. NextScripts: Social Networks Auto-Poster: When you publish something new, this free WordPress plugin will automatically publish it onto multiple social networks.

Site Management

44. Uptime Robot: Monitors your website and informs you when it is down, for free.

45. Filezilla: My favorite FTP client that's 100% free.

46. Gtmetrix: Analyze your website's speed and performance and makes recommendations on how to improve it.

47. Google Alerts: Get alerted when your keywords/ website name is mentioned on the web.

48. Updraft Plus: Backup your website.. don't take a risk that you should not be taking.

49. Google Webmaster Tools: Mostly allows you to see what keywords you are ranking for, add your sitemap and to be notified on anything Google wants to tell you with regards to your website.

50. PopupAlly: Craft free and beautiful popups for your website.

List of the top blogs from 2018

What are the most profitable blogs thus far this year

CPSIA information can be obtained
at www.ICGtesting.com
Printed in the USA
LVHW042247200120
644180LV00014B/906